𝒴ukon Memories

A MOUNTIE'S STORY

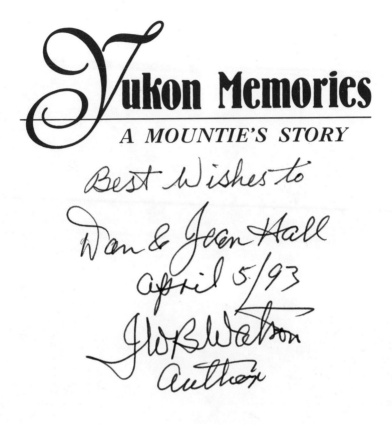

Best Wishes to

Dan & Jean Hall

april 5/93

Floss B Watson

author

Yukon Memories

A MOUNTIE'S STORY

By Jack (Tich) Watson
with Gray Campbell

WHITECAP BOOKS/Vancouver/Toronto

Edited by Marlyn Horsdal
Cover and interior design by Carolyn Deby
Cover illustration by Carolyn Deby
Typeset by CompuType, Vancouver, B.C.

Printed and bound in Canada by D.W. Friesen and Sons Ltd., Altona, Manitoba

Canadian Cataloguing in Publication Data

Watson, Tich.
  Yukon memories

  Includes index.
  ISBN 1-55110-052-5

  1. Watson, Tich. 2. Royal Canadian Mounted Police—Biography. 3. Yukon Territory—Biography. 4. Frontier and pioneer life—Yukon Territory.
  I. Campbell, Gray, 1912-
  II. Title
  HV7911.W38A3 1993   363.2′092   C93-091081-8

The publisher acknowledges the assistance of the Canada Council and the Cultural Services Branch of the government of British Columbia in making this publication possible.

Contents

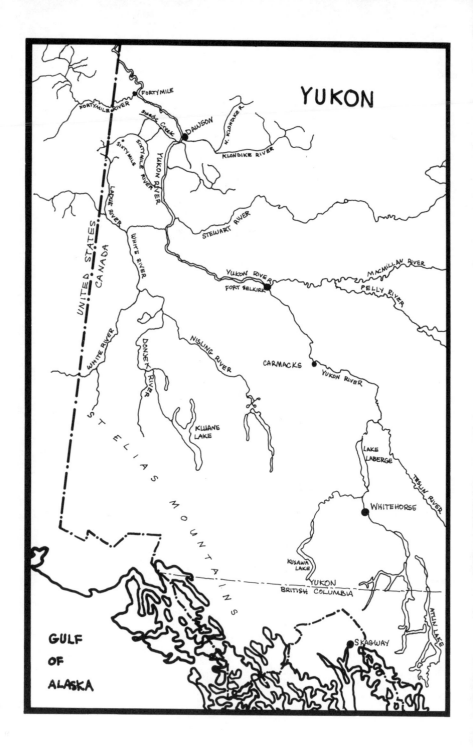

Introduction

"*. . . The men from 'G' Division patrol
the vast areas of the North West Territories and Yukon,
dealing very often with Indians and Eskimos whose knowledge
of the white men's law is rudimentary and who see in a
Mounted Policeman the very agent of the King himself, an
infallible upholder of justice. Here is no haven for the
policeman of the strong arm, the bullying voice, the aggressive
countenance. Here is the opportunity for diplomacy, wisdom,
and the patient capacity of the teacher . . . . Here is the
demand for courage in facing loneliness, in travelling the far
snow-swept trails, in making plain and enforcing the law
with unbending determination . . . ."*

THE OTTAWA JOURNAL (CIRCA 1950)

he Yukon. A huge, wedge-
shaped chunk of Canadian
territory. Bounded by Alaska to the west, the North-
west Territories to the east, British Columbia to the south
and the Beaufort Sea to the north. More than 200,000
square miles of raw, mountainous terrain, far from the
big cities of industrialized Canada. A home to Indians,
invaded by explorers, traders, trappers, prospectors and
missionaries. Supplies and communication from ''outside'' relied upon the mighty Yukon River draining from

the St. Elias range in the south, flowing to the Bering Sea in the northwest: two thousand miles. . . .

Sixty years ago, fresh out from England, I had enlisted in the Royal Canadian Mounted Police. My father, a coal miner, had died in 1922, a comparatively young man, and I had to help mother make a go of it. At 13 I had passed an exemption exam so I could leave school and go to work. I earned small amounts driving cattle to market, doing farm chores, selling newspapers and working in a printing shop. The future looked bleak and to lighten mother's load I had to break away from home. As a member of the Boys Brigade, a semi-military organization like the Boy Scouts, I was assisted in emigrating to Canada where I was trained on a farm.

While the Great Depression set in and the Dirty Thirties ruined the chances of any success in farming, I heard that the nephew of some friends had joined the RCMP. If this lad from eastern Canada could get in, perhaps I had a chance. I made some enquiries, passed the test and landed in Regina, Saskatchewan, in one of three new squads of recruits.

Recruit training was six months and they hammered us into shape through drills, lectures and a very tough riding school. Towards the end of training we examined the bulletin board anxiously to see where our future might lie. One day I noticed that Wally Truitt was posted to the Yukon. He was an outstanding athlete, on the soccer and rugby teams.

"That's a crime, sending Wally to the Yukon," I announced. "There's no sports up there. I'd rather be sent than see Wally go."

The next day I checked the board and Wally's name had been removed. Mine was listed. All members detailed for the Yukon were to report to stores, hand in their kit and leave on Monday. I managed a weekend pass on Friday, went to Winnipeg, got engaged to Mary Ellen Trower, nicknamed "Nellie," and returned to Depot in time to leave for Vancouver by train with the detail on Monday.

I did not see Nellie for another five years.

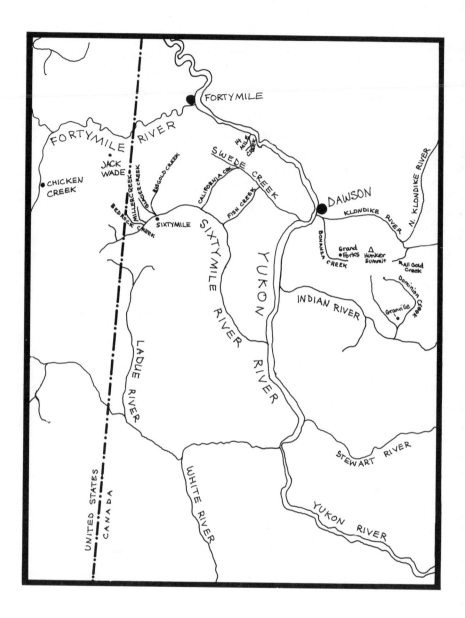

Barney West

CHAPTER ONE

*I*t was June 1932 when the paddle-wheel steamer from Whitehorse, the first of the season, rounded the bend and I caught my first sight of Dawson City. There was a long wooden wharf with freight sheds lining it. Hidden behind it were streets with office buildings, stores and rows of wooden houses. Standing out most prominently was the hospital, at the base of the mountain slide which had occurred before the Gold Rush and was mentioned in native folklore. In the background was the Dome, which towered over the scene. The hospital was run by the sisters of the Grey Nuns. I had arrived in Dawson, via Skagway, Alaska, a scant 34 years after the Gold Rush and as I made my way ashore I wondered what part I would play in the continuing drama of challenge, and possibly adventure, in the years ahead.

I picked up my haversack and went to the barracks, headquarters of the Division which consisted of a superintendent, an inspector, a sergeant major, three sergeants, one corporal and 15 constables. They all seemed too busy to do more than stare at this newcomer as I headed for the orderly room.

Sergeant Major Davis glanced up, nodded a brief welcome and issued his first orders.

"Watson, drop your kit on an empty bed. Change into brown serge and get over to the jail. You are to assist Constable Thornton in supervising the death watch."

Before I had time to unpack, there I was, second in command of the primitive lock-up, guarding a character waiting to be hung for murder. The guard changed every four hours so there was a constant watch on the doomed man's cell. I started to worry at what might lie ahead in this raw and untamed land. I had just turned 23 and was still feeling the bumps and bruises of Depot's drill and riding schools, mixed with a tinge of sadness for my home another world away.

Here I was on my first real assignment, getting to know a man convicted of murder and about to depart this life. I watched him eat his meals, saw that he was escorted to the toilet and observed him playing cribbage, sliding the cards to the guard through the small opening in his cell.

Barney West had been a popular member of the community. It was said that he had been a capable chef in New York and had drifted into the Yukon where he worked as camp cook for a gold-mining company near Dawson. He rented a cabin in town during the winter months, was a heavy drinker and was usually short of money.

One winter he found himself in the police cells, a guest for three months, convicted of stealing money for booze. Prisoners were put to work in those days and Barney's job was chore boy, washing dishes. After making a few pointed culinary suggestions to the cook, he was handed the apron and utensils and told to get on with it. The barracks cook turned in disgust to Barney's place at the sink, to the great delight of the constables. They were sorry when Barney completed his sentence and the regular cook took over again.

On the night of May 10, 1932, Barney West was arrested again. Next day *The Dawson News* ran the following:

Dawson
SCENE OF REVOLTING CRIME—OLD TIMER MURDERED FOR HIS MONEY

Tuesday, May 10, will long be remembered as the day when the horribly mutilated remains of Michael Ligue Essanasa were discovered lying cross-wise on the bed in the cottage long occupied by the deceased. The discovery was made by Sgt. H.H. Cronkhite of the Royal Canadian Mounted Police upon being notified by Mrs. Mary Clark-Hendra that she had not seen Mr. Essanasa since April 30 . . . .

Barney had been drinking with the victim and several others. It was known that Essanasa had been wearing a money belt which was not found at the scene and that West had paid off quite a few debts in town and had purchased jewellery for a lady friend, Marie Tomoff, whom I was to meet later in my career. Constable Jimmy Ward, who had worked on the case, told me the evidence in the cabin indicated the victim had put up quite a fight. They found the murder weapon after draining a slough with the fire department's pumper truck. It was described by Jimmy Ballantine Jr., son of the fire chief, as a sock made of moosehide filled with buckshot.

The jury of six took about 20 minutes to come to a decision of guilty. Mr. Justice C.D. MacAuley sentenced Barney to death by hanging on Tuesday, September 27, 1932. Names of the jury, long-time members of the community, will be remembered by many of today's sourdoughs. They were E.E. Hickey, E. Chapman, H. Gleaves, J. Halliburton, M. McCuish and M. McKinnon.

I had the unenviable duty of seeing this grim sentence carried through to the end. It had been many years since the last hanging at Dawson and a new scaffold had to be constructed. A citizen of the town, Fred Hickling, who was an experienced carpenter, was hired and his assistant was special constable Alec Craig. They erected the scaffold behind the storage buildings and the stables so it would be screened from the public. It had the traditional 13 steps.

The official hangman arrived from the south incognito, mysterious and uncommunicative. The Canadian hangman was always known as "Mr. Ellis," background unknown, and his grey presence remained unobtrusively in the background. After he had inspected the site of the gallows, two members of the detachment were instructed to dig a trench six feet wide, eight feet long and three feet deep. I am sure this pair, when they signed their engagement papers, had no idea they would be digging the grave of a condemned man through permafrost in the Yukon below a scaffold.

As the execution day set by the court drew near, Dr. Nunn, the police surgeon, and Mr. Ellis were escorted to the "Bull Pen" and locked in there before the prisoner was brought from his cell. I watched the scene as the two friends met.

"How are you feeling, Barney?"

"Pretty good, Doc, under the circumstances," Barney replied.

Dr. Nunn took his pulse.

"Would you like a cigar?"

"I sure would enjoy a good smoke, at least."

While this was going on Mr. Ellis remained in the background, behind Barney, making a note of his height and estimating his weight. The result was a decision by Mr. Ellis that the drop would have to be increased, which meant the boys had to dig another two feet into the permafrost.

True to his word, the good doctor sent in a large cigar and the aroma permeated the jail. It took Barney two days to finish it, and watching him relish this luxury caused me to wonder what he was thinking. He treated that cigar with great care, setting it aside carefully to finish next day.

Mr. Ellis was busy in another direction. He had been lubricating a rope about an inch thick to make it pliable for curling and knotting. It was fastened to the wall at the end of the corridor at headquarters and extended about 60 feet to the other end of the passage. Every member of the force was thus caught up in the macabre drama, for they had to slide under the rope to enter their offices.

There had been a certain admiration building for the attitude of the doomed man. He had never complained about the treatment or the food, which was the same as we had to suffer. Only once did he ask if something could be done to help him sleep. The light over the table of the night guard shone into his eyes and a suspended piece of paper provided sufficient shade.

On Barney's last day Dr. Nunn visited the prisoner in the "Bull Pen" for a final check. Standing six feet away I heard the conversation.

"Barney, would you like a drink?"

"Yes I would, Doc, more than anything."

Dr. Nunn produced a very large glass and a full bottle of Johnnie Walker. Barney held it to the light with reverence, almost filled the tumbler with scotch and held it out as a toast.

"Johnnie Walker, you son-of-a-bitch. You got me into this. Now see me through to the end."

Barney put the glass to his lips and slowly emptied it of its contents. He was a real professional tippler because he did not bat an eye. Mr. Ellis entered and quickly fastened Barney's wrists   with a leather strap. Then he placed an ebony rod behind his back, tucked into the crotch of his elbows and securely locking his arms. Mr. Ellis was coldly efficient, his actions quicker than the time it has taken to read this.

The drill required two members of the force to escort Barney from the jail to the scaffold, a distance of about 40 yards. Barney did not waste any time going to his doom. He was half a step ahead of the escort, quickly mounted the 13 steps to the scaffold and stood ready.

Mr. Ellis, holding a black cloth hood, asked Barney if he had anything to say.

"Do you have to put that thing on me?"

"Yes I do," Mr. Ellis replied.

"Then make it snappy," said Barney.

In a flash the hood was on, followed by the noose, and the trap door sprung.

For several days there was a strange quietness in barracks. As the weeks passed, patrols and investigations kept us busy. Those who had completed their four years in the Yukon went "outside" on transfers and gradually the new arrivals who came to fill the vacancies helped put thoughts of Barney out of everyone's mind.

I was relieved of my duties and stood ready to meet the next challenge. My introduction to northern service had started with an unfortunate, shattering experience since I had been in such close proximity to the final days of Barney West. It probably had affected me more than the others, but with the resilience of youth I managed to settle down to a more normal routine. There were stables, night guard, local investigations, escorts, court and, when we needed exercise, we had our own form of soccer.

There would only be enough of us off duty at any time to make four or five a side, but we'd trot out with the ball to a grassy area beside the paddocks, place a couple of stable jackets for a goal and away we'd go. That is how I picked up my nickname.

One day we were just getting warmed up and I was attacking the goal when Jerry Webb, defending, stood as I swerved and swept past. I was going full speed and just when I thought I was clear he deliberately tripped me and I went flying. When I got to my feet I was boiling, and as I approached Jerry with raised fists, he said,

"Oh, for Christ sakes, Tich, you looked so darn

funny the way you were running. Made me think of Little Tich, the English comedian. Sorry, old chap.''

They were all laughing. I stood there feeling foolish, but still indignant as I cooled off. Jerry offered his hand and I shook it. Unfortunately the ''Tich'' stuck and followed me through my years in northern service.

In the stables we had a fine work team of blacks to haul supplies and a couple of saddle horses. Mounted patrols were on the back burner while the Barney West death watch went on. I had always liked horses and got along with them even as a child.

Of the two saddle horses, I was particularly taken with a fine-looking filly, a chestnut of average height that stood beautifully and moved like a trained polo pony. Of course she had been assigned to the superintendent, Freddy Allard.

One day I was leaning over the fence, watching her move daintily and I called her name, ''Kitty.'' She looked up and I waved and called her over. Without hesitating she came to the fence and put her head over so I could nuzzle and talk to her. Behind my back Freddy Allard was walking from the officers' quarters to his office. He turned to approach and called out in his French-Canadian accent.

''You like my little 'orse?''

''Yes sir,'' I replied, standing at attention. ''She's a fine-looking, lively and affectionate pony.''

''Then you shall ride her,'' he said, and went on his way.

A few days later I was told the sergeant major wanted to see me. I cleaned up and reported.

''Watson, we are resuming mounted patrols. Your

mount is Kitty. Constable Harrington will ride Darby. You will take turns patrolling the creeks.''

I got in touch with Pat Harrington and we planned alternate patrols over varying routes to cover the territory. We would go out for six or eight days at a time, return from each patrol for a day to rest and write our reports, then we would do a week on town station. This involved patrolling Dawson day and night, checking people, businesses and residences. The main concern was fire, catching any outbreak in time.

We would usually start the mounted patrol by riding four miles east into the gold-mining area and up Bonanza Creek 15 or 20 miles, then climb to Hunker Summit and branch off from there. We made a point of stopping at every shack or camp, picking up news and gossip, and checking on the health, supplies and mental attitudes of the single men isolated nearly year-round. We usually stopped overnight at roadhouses which catered to riders and their mounts in rough fashion. No crimes were reported during the months I spent on this duty, and I like to think that our visits and presence helped.

We watched several gold dredges operating and observed hundreds of men shovelling gravel into sluice boxes on many private claims. The water carried away the small gravel while the gold was caught in the riffles. Just before twilight the day's gold would be removed and taken to the log cabins. The small operators had their own methods of security, while the larger outfits placed their gold in iron strong-boxes.

It was an interesting job in pleasant weather and again I seemed to have the breaks. Kitty, in addition to her fine appearance, was intelligent and an easy ride, and could go to a smooth canter from a standstill. Pat's mount, Darby, had a broken nose and was sluggish in comparison. I suspect he might have been a problem with the mounted troop in Vancouver and had been banished north.

Early in October 1932, I rode into Dawson just before dinner, tired and hungry after a dusty week, for it seldom rained in that part of the Yukon. After unsaddling, watering and feeding Kitty I had to report to the sergeant major. I had spent the last weary miles dreaming of a hot supper and bath, then crawling into bed for a well-earned night's sleep. The sergeant major shattered my reverie with crisp, clear orders.

"Get your written report to Sergeant Cronkhite early in the morning," he said, "and be prepared to leave for Vancouver on the steamer *Keno* for escort duty. Full review order."

That meant red serge with buttons gleaming, Sam Browne belt with side-arms, and riding boots polished to pass parade-ground inspection. Bone weary, I spent the early evening writing my report. Then I tackled my breeches, giving them a good brushing and a shake to get rid of the dust. I unfolded my red serge and polished the buttons and badges. My riding boots were a mess, caked with Kitty's sweat and grimed with dust from the trails. I did the best I could with saddle soap and elbow grease until I couldn't keep my eyes open. I put the boots aside and climbed into bed, hoping they would be dry enough in the morning to take the polish.

At 9:00 A.M. I stood in front of Sergeant Cronkhite in review order. He had been serving in the Yukon for nine years and had an enviable service record. He was strict but fair. He gazed at me without a smile or comment, starting with the leather band on my stetson, working his eyes over the buttons and side-arms and pausing at my boots while I held my breath. He had been through it in his day and probably realized I had done my best under the circumstances, for he picked up my patrol report and glanced over it without a word. He obviously had something else on his mind.

"You will be leaving on the afternoon boat for White-horse, escorting a female patient for the mental hospital in Vancouver. Your party will be met at Whitehorse and taken to the barracks along with the matron, a nurse named Hollis, until just before the train leaves for Skagway."

He gave me time to digest this new role, and when I nodded he went on with the briefing.

"Your passage from Skagway to Vancouver has been arranged. Pick up your tickets before leaving Dawson. At Vancouver you will be met and taken immediately to the mental hospital. There you will deliver the prisoner with documents and receive a receipt which you will attach to your report on return."

He paused again and allowed a smile. We both relaxed. Then he said, not unkindly, "Watson, I presume you know what happens if you lose your prisoner."

"Yes, sergeant," I gulped, and remembered the horror story. A couple of years before, two members were taking a prisoner to the penitentiary. In an unguarded moment the man leaped overboard and disappeared into the swift-flowing, icy Yukon River. The escorts, in red serge with boots and spurs and side-arms, knew they would not survive if they jumped overboard to attempt recapture. In short order they faced a court martial and were dismissed from the force in disgrace.

Wishing me good luck, he handed over written instructions:

Two cabins have been reserved for your party. Miss Hollis and Mrs. Marie Tomoff will sleep in one cabin and you will occupy the one immediately adjoining. Should Miss Hollis require assistance she will call you by knocking on the wall separating the two cabins.

The Escort

CHAPTER TWO

As this was my first escort duty I did not know what to expect. My first thought was that perhaps I was getting this trip in appreciation for the long hours I had spent in the saddle. I know now that nothing like that could ever happen. It was simply a duty to perform and I was conveniently next on the roster. I had time to pack and ponder. Maybe I was lucky. I had always admired nurses, so smart and attractive. I was looking forward to meeting Miss Hollis and I was in for another surprise.

Miss Hollis (she never told me her first name) was thin and stand-offish, about 90 pounds of distaste. Marie Tomoff, by contrast, was a ponderous 200-pounder accustomed to looking after herself in her questionable chosen profession. Shades of Barney West, she was the one on whom he had spent his ill-gotten loot, for jewellery. Her husband had a restaurant in Dawson and he would complain to the police when Marie wandered off; they would find her in the creeks visiting the miners. He divorced her and her actions became so erratic she was committed with apparently suicidal tendencies. I was not really surprised when Miss Hollis sputtered at the outset, "Constable Watson, I am not staying alone with that woman."

I could appreciate her concern. If this mental patient decided to commit suicide, she could sweep the little nurse aside, or take her along. One step outside and she'd be over the rail. I would be helpless in the adjoining cabin, even if I were fully awake. I tried to calm Miss Hollis with assurances that I would devise a better plan.

The *Keno* was a stern-wheel paddle steamer. The main deck was for freight and the wood to heat the boilers. The upper deck had very small cabins with partitions so thin you could pick up the conversation in the adjoining one. While I was trying to adjust to the situation, Marie Tomoff decided to complicate matters, saying she refused to eat with the other passengers. This suited Miss Hollis just fine for she enjoyed dining and socializing with the passengers, temporarily free of responsibility, and took her time about it. This left the two of us eating in their cabin in a state of silent, apprehensive hostility.

At bedtime I stood outside the cabin while prisoner and nurse prepared to retire. After the ladies had had time to get settled I entered the cabin, placed the wicker chair against the door and tried to make myself comfortable. I felt sure Marie could not slip through the two-foot window without waking me, if I should doze.

It was a long, uncomfortable night. I welcomed the dawn when I could step outside to fill my lungs with fresh air and stretch my legs, which were still encased in tight riding boots. After the long, sleepless night with little chance to freshen up, I began to wonder just what I had done to deserve this. I could feel the tension, even hostility, from the patient and the cool silence of the nurse. Only mealtime gave little Miss Hollis a chance to escape. In the morning and afternoon we walked gingerly along the deck, Miss Hollis next to the rail and I very close behind.

The second evening we repeated the drill but I was determined to ease the strait-jacket of review order. I loosened my side-arms, unbuttoned the red serge and unlaced the riding boots, to aid the circulation in my legs for the first time in 36 hours. Then I settled more comfortably in the wicker chair.

The hours passed slowly. The only sound was the throb of the engine and the vibration of the vessel under way, which caused me to doze occasionally. During one of these moments I surfaced with a peculiar sensation of something stirring the air in front of my face. I felt my head and shoulders, fanned the air in front, felt nothing in the dark, and relaxed once more.

Some time later I became alert to the same sensation, checked the space around me in the quiet dark without result and began to wonder if I had been dreaming. There was not a sound in the cabin and no movement. Concluding I was overtired and imagining things, I tried to settle back and relax, longing for daylight.

The minutes slowly ticked away and my tension eased, but not for long. Something soft and fleshy brushed across my face and I jumped up to snap on the light. There was the delightful Mrs. Tomoff in the buff, without a stitch to cover her 200 pounds, trying to ease out of the upper bunk in that tiny cabin without disturbing the matron. It must have been her foot searching for a step that had alerted me. I hauled off and laid a good slap on her backside with a gruff order not to try that again. She made no further attempt to escape.

That was just as well, for I began to wonder how long I could keep this up and I had to face another long night of strain. We managed to pull through, though it still seems like a nightmare, and on the fourth day we arrived at Whitehorse. We were met by a police vehicle and driver and whisked to the safety of the barracks where I had my first real chance to freshen and loosen up.

Expecting to catch the train for Skagway in about an hour, I was preparing myself mentally for what might lie ahead when I was informed my party would be staying overnight at the barracks and I was temporarily relieved of my responsibilities. No reason was given for the change in plans, but later I learned that Judge MacAuley had also been a passenger on the *Keno* and had telephoned the commanding officer at Whitehorse. He reported that I had not slept for three nights and had been through a bad time. Relieved of the tension and strain for a dozen hours, I could have slept through an earthquake.

It was a different world next morning with prisoner and matron in a better mood, enjoying the legendary White Pass railroad run to Skagway through the breathtaking scenery. From the train we were quickly transferred to a Canadian Pacific steamship for the delightful cruise down the Inside Passage to Vancouver. This part of the journey was a piece of cake, a lovely canter, five days of bliss with all the hurdles left behind in the Yukon. We had been given cabins deep down in the ship, inside ones with no portholes. Miss Hollis had a key which allowed her to lock them in and I had the adjoining cabin. The patient was in a more placid mood and with responsibility eased, I could even enjoy the meals.

A police vehicle met us at dockside in Vancouver and transported us directly to the hospital, where I was relieved of my charge and handed the required receipt. Miss Hollis, having completed her contract nursing in the Yukon, had worked her passage "outside" and we parted, she to find another assignment. I reported to the sergeant major at Fairmont Barracks, who arranged for my accommodation, and was granted a week's leave.

I enjoyed the reunion with the men in barracks, many of whom I had trained with at Regina, and being shown the sights of the fascinating city. It was a refreshing change from the frontier rawness of Dawson, but curiously, after a week of this, I was ready and anxious to return north. As I began to feel its pull I understood why the old-timers advised recruits that four years was enough before it "got hold of you !" I wanted to taste the rest of it, test myself against the obstacles of winter and rugged terrain, learning the craft and sharing the adventures of police work.

With no responsibility, my return journey was a bonus holiday all the way through the Inside Passage and over the mountains to Whitehorse. But there the holiday ended. I noticed the river steamers had been pulled ashore, skidded on to 12- by 12-foot timbers by steam winches and lined up ten feet apart where they would remain until spring. Ice was moving quickly downstream; winter was setting in and I began to wonder how I would make it back to Dawson.

I checked into barracks and learned that the following morning I would travel overland with the Royal Mail, which in those days was carried on a sleigh pulled by a caterpillar tractor. It had not entered my mind that the return journey would be any different from the trip south, and I only had a pea-jacket to cover my dress uniform when I needed a buffalo coat. I should have been wearing moccasins and mukluks instead of riding boots, and the muskrat-fur cap instead of my stetson. Fortunately I was able to borrow a cap or I'd have reached Dawson with frozen ears, if not a frozen brain.

It wasn't with a light heart that I started out on my first overland trek in winter. I should have been thinking ahead. "Experience is a great teacher," it has been said and I had just joined the class as the youngest pupil.

We started the trek soon after daylight and I estimated the overland journey would be about 300 miles. The land route tried to avoid obstacles by following the contours, climbing and descending the undulating trail. At times it went 20 or 30 miles inland to shorten the distance along the winding Yukon River. Extreme cold had not yet set in but sometimes there was a cutting wind and perhaps 20 degrees of frost. Riding the sleigh was too cold so I walked to keep warm, jumping on the load of mail bags only when we had to climb a hill. The leather in my riding boots became stiff as boards and my feet and legs took a beating. In addition to the driver there was another passenger, an experienced sourdough with sensible footwear, and how I longed for moccasins and mukluks like his. He also preferred to walk and we helped keep each other going when we were fighting cold and fatigue.

We reached the first river crossing at Carmacks and the three of us unloaded the mail and our luggage, which we carried down the bank to the landing. The mailman signalled and we waited patiently until eventually a canoe pushed off from the far shore. It was an education to watch a native Indian paddle upstream, threading his way across the fast-flowing river, dodging chunks of moving ice to reach our landing. We carefully loaded a third of the sacks and my fellow passenger stepped gingerly aboard for the first crossing. The Indian unloaded passenger and mail and I crossed with the next load. The two of us struggled to carry the freight up a steep bank about 12 feet high and on to another sleigh while the mailman came over with the third load.

With everything on board, packed and secure, we plodded on behind the second tractor and sleigh in a grey landscape. A chill wind made sure we did not over-heat. Mile after mile we tramped, burning up energy and building up our appetites until we came to the first roadhouse on the old trail. This promised to take the cold out of our bones, return the feeling to feet and hands, fill the hollow in our tummies.

It was a typical Yukon roadhouse built of logs, about 20 feet wide and twice as long. At one end on the ground floor there were two single cots used by the husband and wife who operated this lonely haven. They had a large, cast-iron cookstove and also a heater, made from a 45-gallon oil drum, raised off the floor by flat stones. A large pile of firewood was stacked nearby. Several home-made easy chairs gave the cabin a cosy look and there was a small radio on a shelf, though it seldom picked up clear reception.

A small table behind the stove held an enamel wash

basin, and a well-used towel hung on a nail, close enough to dry quickly from the cookstove as everyone used it in turn. Toilet facilities were outside in an unheated, two-hole, well-ventilated "biffy." No one was tempted to linger over the harness or underwear sections in Eaton's catalogue.

Guests slept on the second floor, a long, plain room without partitions, with a very small window at each end and simple cots on the board floor. There were no rugs or carpets. Some travellers packed their own sleeping bags but there were clean sheets and a pile of blankets, which often needed shaking, for those who needed them.

By the time we had thawed out and washed we began to absorb the snug atmosphere of the warm cabin. The fragrance of freshly baked bread mingled with the aroma of roast moose which had just emerged from the oven. We tackled this feast with old-fashioned gusto and washed it down with mugs of hot, strong coffee. When we dragged ourselves upstairs to the cots we didn't need rocking.

All along the winter route from Whitehorse to Dawson there were similar roadhouses for stops both at noon and overnight, a chance to thaw out twice a day. The food was usually in the same style with home-made bread or buns, meat and potatoes at each meal. It took four days to travel the distance, and though it had not been dangerous or too arduous an experience, I was overjoyed when I reached the barracks and could relish my own bed with the luxury of a hot bath.

After making a complete report of the escort trip "outside," I settled down to the duties of town station interspersed with the freedom of patrols for a week or so at a time, riding the smooth and affectionate Kitty. It was a break from discipline and in fine weather I considered it the best job in the world. Generally considered the two most popular roadhouses for overnight were Hunker Summit, operated by Mr. Fournier, and Granville, where Andrew Taddie and Gertie Melhouse always made us welcome and provided excellent fare. The proprietors were a reliable source of information, as they knew everyone either settled in the district or passing through. They were shrewd in assessing physical or mental attitudes and if any problems were brewing. I began to meet a lot of friendly, pleasant, hard-working characters and began to pick up the unique, fraternal spirit of the Yukon. I did not realize it at the time but the examples of unselfish co-operation spelled it out for me. It consisted of thinking about the next stranger to come along the trail, and knowing how survival depended upon sharing and caring.

When the cooler weather turned into Yukon winter that first year, it became so cold I began to wish someone else had the horse and I could keep the fires going back in barracks. To protect my hands from freezing while riding, I would take turns placing each one in its wool and leather mitt under the opposite armpit, holding the reins in the other hand. Then I would briskly rub my knees to restore circulation, transfer the reins to the warmed hand and repeat. The buffalo coat and muskrat-fur cap with ear flaps were life-savers, as horse and rider pushed on through the wall of penetrating cold until we reached the roadhouse where we could both get under cover. We kept close tab on the temperature, for our orders were clear. Whenever the thermometer dropped lower than 54 degrees below zero the horse was to remain in the barn. On two consecutive days I rode in 48 below. Kitty had grown her own winter coat.

Between horse patrols, when I was back on normal duties, I began to get interested in the dog team. The kennels were in the compound adjacent to the stables. I would hang around watching the trainer feeding them and taking them out for a run. Sometimes I'd ask a question or lend a hand, as feeding, harnessing, positioning the sleigh and the words of command were all new to me.

Corporal Delaney was an accomplished dog man but a bit of a loner and very quiet around the barracks, preferring his own company. One day he walked through the room and surprised me by stopping at my bed.

"Watty, I'm going to take the dogs for a run. Want to come?"

"Sure would, corp," I replied, jumping up.

"Grab your gear then, and give me a hand."

We dragged out the sleigh first, placing the front runners on either side of a special hitching post. Then I watched Delaney string out the harness, hooked to the sleigh, for the six dogs. I listened to the way he spoke to them and watched his actions as he first brought the wheel dog and hooked it independently of the others. This was to enable it to jump the traces and swing sharply if the sleigh was heading for danger. The next four dogs were brought out in turn, placed in their collars and hooked in line. The lead dog came last and by this time they were all jumping up and down in excitement, their tails waving aloft, and yipping eagerly. They loved to work. Having placed a canvas in the carryall for me, Delaney was ready to go.

"Jump in, Watty," he called, and I nipped into place,

with a grip on the sides as he pulled the sleigh back from the restraining post and leaped onto a runner. With joyous sounds the dogs took off at full speed, not needing a word of command, while the corporal pressed his foot hard on the brake, sending up a plume of snow. After the initial burst of speed they settled down to a steady pace and we relaxed as we headed out into the country.

I made six trips as a passenger, helping Delaney a bit more each time and picking up the drill. Then I was detailed to feed the team, who gradually began to accept me, and I became a familiar sight around the kennels. Until one day I walked into Sergeant Cronkhite's office.

"Sergeant, is it possible for me to take the dogs out by myself?"

"Try a short run. See how you manage. Let me know how you make out."

It would not matter to Delaney. They weren't his team. He was a very experienced detachment man who had finished his tour, was waiting to be posted "outside" and had been putting in time. I dressed carefully and walked out to the kennels, excited but slightly apprehensive. Would this team, part wolf, accept me and co-operate? They were by no means cuddly pets.

I tried to imitate the corporal's movements and voice as I placed the sleigh firmly against the post, laid out the harness and hauled out the wheel dog. No problem there, as he was anxious to get hooked up, and the others began to show excitement at the chance for a run. As they were hitched up in turn, and finally the lead dog, they were showing increased impatience by jumping into their collars. Eager to run, they weren't waiting for any command.

I managed to calm the leader long enough to free the sleigh from the post, jump aboard the runner and press hard on the brake. I'll never forget this first solo departure. The team tore out of the gate in high gear and because I was pressing the brake with all my strength, the hard-packed snow sent up a spray of white. I was further impressed with the strength of the brutes.

They came out on the main road through town and before I could think, the leader decided to make a sharp turn to the right, with the rest of the dogs strung out and making a frantic attempt to keep up. When the sleigh reached the turn it whipped 90 degrees, shot out from under my feet and tipped over. In desperation I retained a death grip on it. I was flipped over on my back and dragged for several blocks through Dawson before the team heeded my calls to halt. As I cleared the white mask of snow from my eyes, nostrils and mouth I could see the smiles on the faces of the old-timers standing on the wooden sidewalk. I set the sleigh upright, calmed the dogs down and made a more sedate start, which took us clear of the town before they settled down to their regular pace.

On the next attempt I made sure I had the problem licked. They weren't going to upset the outfit and dump me again. Instead of balancing on a runner fighting the brake, I would free the toboggan from the post, jump firmly in and sit tight, hanging onto the rope attached to the cross members, and this time there would be no tipping.

We made a normal start and I hung on grimly, so sure of success I was ready for whatever the leader decided when we hit the main road. He turned sharply to the right; the toboggan twisted flatly sideways as it skidded across the hard-packed snow and hit a solid bank. It decelerated so quickly it jarred me loose and I kept on going into the snow while the team went on their merry way.

I was furious as I fought my way out of the bank and on to my feet, so mad I never noticed if anyone was watching. I had to hike several miles out of town before I found the team, badly tangled in the harness. The only thought I had was to get the blasted brutes back to the kennels before anyone reported what had happened; I'd leave them there and turn my energy to better use. As a dog-team driver, I was a washout.

After a few days and some words of fellowship and understanding from the veterans in barracks, my sense of failure began to evaporate and I could not resist the desire to try and handle the team once again.

Gradually I learned how to manage and understand these lovely animals who had tried me so sorely. I frequently drove them east to a roadhouse at a place called Arlington, operated by the Skistead family, about 15 miles from town. After a short visit over a cup of coffee, with the dogs rested and ready for the run back, it was a sport tinged with sheer joy. The team loved these outings, and so did I, the bruises and indignities filed and forgiven. I was just about ready for a real test.

Raefe Douthwaite

CHAPTER THREE

*C*oming in from a sparkling run with the team one sunny day, I floated over the snow from kennels to barracks, bursting with rude health and with ''feathers in my boots'' as Carcoux, the Regina trumpeter, used to say. As I entered barracks Sergeant Major Davies intercepted me.

''Change into uniform and report to my office. The officer commanding wishes to see you.''

My bubble of joy popped and worry set in. What had I done to cause being paraded before the O.C.? Then I calmed down as I could not think of anything worse than the mistakes I had made with the dogs and had not reported. Superintendent Tommy Caulkin, who had replaced Allard, was the very model of a northern man, respected by all for his experiences that had gone into the annals of the force. History books included his

Bathurst Inlet patrol, which had survived in spite of a sled break-down, with their clothing in rags, living on a diet of dog flesh, and fighting arctic cold, wolves and rebellious natives. With Inspector French ill, then-Sergeant Major Caulkin bore the strain and got them all through. Now our superintendent, this was the man who had my future in his hands. He quickly put me at ease, asking for details of my patrols and escort duties. Then he got down to business.

"Watson, Kitty, your saddle horse, has been sold. I understand you have been practising with the dog team. How are you making out?"

"A shaky start, sir, but improving each time though I haven't tried running cross country."

"I'd like to know if you'd be interested in making a patrol with Corporal Douthwaite."

"Sir, I would appreciate the opportunity."

"You'll get a chance to learn from an experienced veteran who's skilled in survival, to search for a missing trapper near the International Boundary."

Not knowing what to say I stood for seconds, dazed.

"Any questions?"

"No sir."

"Right. Report to Douthwaite. Take your instructions from him, and good luck," he added with a smile.

I stepped back one pace, saluted, and left with a light heart. Excited at the opportunity for adventure so early in my career, I raced up the stairs to find the corporal, who had a room of his own. I had met him some months before, a handsome, seasoned northern man, ruggedly well built and of average height. He had the bearing and accent of an educated Englishman, reserved but friendly. Yet he had a wicked sense of humour, as well I remember. One day I had a deaf plumber working on a water main outside the barracks; the plumber was in the excavation and I was bent over handing him the tools he needed. Corporal Douthwaite was up on the second floor when he spotted me in this awkward position, reaching down with a wrench, my backside a perfect target. He grabbed his Webley air pistol and scored a bull's eye. My explosive shout penetrated the deaf plumber's head as he turned to look up in surprise. This was the man who was to be my mentor.

He seemed pleased that I was to be his partner on the patrol and he advised what kit and clothing I would need.

"Get packed and be prepared to leave for Sixtymile at 5:30 tomorrow morning," he said.

Sixtymile was a gold-mining settlement, 60 miles from Dawson as the crow flies, but 80-odd miles by winter trail. I emptied my kit bag and sorted out the items necessary to meet the hazards of the trail in any possible emergency. We had to be self-sufficient in food for ourselves and the dogs. In addition, Raefe had warned me about possible, unsuspected risks.

"Sweating on the run is inevitable," he said, "but you must change into dry underclothes when you stop. And always be ready for a quick change if you happen to fall through the ice."

I went over his list carefully as I laid out extra Stanfield's (two-piece heavy underwear), four pairs of heavy woollen socks, woollen shirts, a civilian windbreaker, a government-issue canvas parka, muskrat-fur cap with flaps that covered the ears, woollen mitts and special gauntlets lined with heavy flannel cloth that came halfway up the forearm.

We wore regulation uniform melton-cloth slacks and over them long black woollen stockings inside moccasins that were inside mukluks. I added toilet articles and extra heavy-duty towels, not realizing until later that we were actually travelling light for what the corporal considered a short run.

We made an early start with the six-dog team, now familiar and friendly as they had helped me learn the drill. I think they sensed this was to be more than an exercise run and were eager to be off. We travelled up the Yukon River on the ice, going south, then turned westerly to run up Swede Creek for about 12 miles, until we found an empty log cabin where Raefe decided to camp. Now my training started under the eyes of a trail-wise veteran.

"I'll get the fire going in the Yukon stove and start the meal," he said. "Look after the dogs and unload." (A Yukon stove is made of sheet metal, in a box shape, 36 inches long, 16 inches wide and the same depth, with a hinged door at the front end, to feed in split logs. Normally it is supported by metal legs, but at this cabin it sat on flat stones, giving it more stability.)

I slipped the animals out of their harness, tied them to well-separated trees and fed them their ration of dried fish. Then I moved our sleeping and kit bags inside, covered one bunk with the corporal's cured caribou skin and spread his sleeping bag. On the other bunk I spread the canvas cover from the toboggan and my own sleeping bag as the cabin began to warm up. By this time the meal was ready, and we tucked into beans with thick sliced bacon and fried bread washed down with hot, strong tea.

I took stock of Raefe's basic equipment. A large

frying pan had several uses. After cooking, snow was scooped up and melted in it and it was used to wash our plates. A gallon tin, which had contained preserved fruit, was made into a pot; its lid was removed and heavy wire inserted to form a handle. In this we made our coffee and tea, bringing the brew just to a boil, and then throwing in a handful of snow to settle the grounds or leaves.

The cleanest snow was usually at the base of small shrubs but in a severe winter rabbits had trouble finding their favourite food and they would resort to eating the bark off the shrubs. The next snowfall would cover their droppings, which managed to get scooped up for the pot of coffee. As the little balls of digested bark floated to the top, they would be easily flipped out with a fork without damaging the brew. It was standard practice.

The temperature was around 20 degrees below zero Fahrenheit and we had travelled some 25 miles, which was not bad for the first day. The cabin was now quite warm and I was ready to stretch out on my bunk. Raefe was in better shape and he too was ready to turn in. But his training and discipline made him set another example.

"We've got to think ahead," he said, picking up his axe. "Open up the sleeping bags so they absorb heat from the stove."

He went outside and chopped down a tree. I followed him out and we dragged it to the cabin where we cut it into stove lengths and split it.

"The cardinal rule on the trail," he said, "is to leave an adequate supply of firewood for the next person coming by."

Back in the cabin Raefe picked up a stick an inch thick. With his hunting knife he carefully shaved three-inch-long curls on both sides, repeated this several times, and laid them carefully aside.

"That'll give us a quick start to our fire in the morning."

"But corp, that's pretty green. Will it burn?"

"No problem this time of year. When it gets this cold the sap flows from the branches into the roots."

Tired though I was, I did not sleep easily. There was no place to fit my hip bone, which kept slipping between the poles. I was used to a soft mattress but found the answer when I made a coil with my top shirt and used it as a cushion.

Before daybreak the corporal was up, making a crackling fire that proved his theory. I watched him dash outside, wash face and hands in a snowbank and hurry inside for a towel rub-down. I followed his example, which proved to be a most invigorating ritual. It was still dark and the snow in the cold air was sharp on bare skin.

Raefe prepared a breakfast of thick slices of bacon and powdered eggs scrambled in melted snow. I packed and loaded the toboggan and fed the dogs, so as soon as the dishes were washed we were ready to hit the trail. But Raefe felt it necessary to point out another lesson for survival.

He took me around to check the wood supply. He explained that this modest cabin, built by a stranger, was left open for the use of any traveller and represented a way of life unique to the Yukon. Built with logs and poles, it had four bare walls and a dirt floor. Two bunks, attached to the walls, were made of three-inch-thick poles three feet off the ground. A six-inch metal stovepipe extended through a Yukon chimney, a 12-inch hole in the roof with metal flashing, leaving an open space between the pipe and the wooden-pole roof, which was chinked with moss and covered with soil. Raefe's message remained with me all my life.

"Always leave a supply of wood for the next traveller and never walk away before making sure your fire has completely burnt out."

We made an easy run on a well-beaten trail, eating up the morning hours and scoring well on the miles when my stomach reminded me it was noon. It was time for another lesson.

"Takes too long to stop, make a fire and prepare a meal."

With Raefe's words we each took a handful of raisins, munching them slowly on the move, and to my surprise I found them adequate to maintain my energy level. We continued up Swede Creek a few more miles, then swung left up a tributary called Fish Creek which led us to a divide. We crossed this into California Creek. Here we found a cabin near its mouth and stayed overnight. I found myself slipping easily into the drill, had a better night's sleep and made a morning dash outside at the same time as Raefe.

We had breakfast, I made the final checks on woodpile and stove and we were quickly away. We were now travelling in the Sixtymile valley, an expanse of low-lying country with hills in the distance. We found two feet of snow on the trail, with two inches of fresh snow on top, but the trail was hard packed below the surface, which made for easy travelling. The dogs ate up the miles as we took turns running behind or riding and we reached Miller Creek late that afternoon. A mile up Miller we came to a log cabin, small but better built than the average. This was Corporal Douthwaite's lone detachment. It consisted of two rooms, a bedroom/office and a kitchen with dining area. There was linoleum on the wooden floor and the cabin had the luxury of both a wood cookstove and a wood heater.

For the next two days Raefe caught up with his office work while I helped prepare for the missing-trapper patrol. I fed the dogs and split wood. Raefe taught me how to prepare rations of partially cooked brown beans. Spread out on cheesecloth outside where they froze individually, they were packed in a sack and stored, sharp-frozen, in the coldest part of the cabin. They would thaw more quickly in the frying pan on the trail in their original shape than they would in a large, solid mass.

While I was doing chores Raefe planned his search pattern and made lists of important items to be stored in the carryall on the toboggan. It was made of tanned moosehide and resembled a bathtub two feet wide, three feet deep and eight feet long. The opening was drawn together with rope, and the packing sequence was most important for safety and survival.

It took us the better part of a day to arrange, sort and pack the carryall. Into the bottom went the frozen dog food; three bundles of dried salmon weighing 45 pounds each. The ration was two pounds a day for each animal. Then we packed 90 pounds of pre-cooked, frozen beans, five pounds of fat pork and 40 pounds of hard-tack biscuits an inch thick.

"The heaviest items first," Raefe said, "to give the load stability in rough going so it won't tip easily."

We added our kit bags with spare clothing for emergencies, two eiderdown sleeping bags and snuggled in tea, coffee, one loaf of bread, a tin of jam, ten pounds of raisins and the matches. Raefe's large frying pan, coffee pot, enamel wash basin, towels, soap and cutlery followed. This we covered with a large canvas, the whole thing fastened securely to the toboggan by a heavy rope weaving back and forth across the load to lace it up.

The last items, which were placed on top, were the 30-30 rifle, a double-bitted axe, the caribou skin and two pairs of snowshoes, one set six feet long, the other four. These were fastened by a fine cord, tied so they could be removed quickly in an emergency.

The missing trapper, Harry Hanlon, had apparently operated in the White River watershed with his base camp about ten miles from the river mouth. He had been missing two years and a search in the area where he normally worked failed to uncover any information or clues. A number of patrols had been made at the eastern end of the river. Now it was decided that a patrol should be made towards the headwaters of the White River as the only other area he might have explored.

When the order came to Douthwaite to prepare and outfit for this search, his detachment had a team of five young dogs. He was just breaking them in and he felt they might not have the stamina to pull a heavy load, climb over a mountain range 5,000 feet high and complete the mission. So he borrowed the older, larger and tougher team of six huskies at Dawson. They were the very team I had been training with and I guess that is how I happened to be selected.

With all preparations checked and double-checked by the meticulous corporal, the day came when we were as ready for the adventure as we would ever be. My feelings for Raefe grew with my respect for his experience and confidence in his decisions. I admired the way he handled the working team and the equipment, his sense of the environment and his reading of the weather, for we had no radio reports to rely upon. Whatever we had to face I felt sure of my partner's competence, and I was as eager to get going on the unknown trail as were the dogs.

The Search

CHAPTER FOUR

*T*he patrol left the detachment early the following morning and the dogs were as excited as I was, waving their bushy tails frantically, bouncing into their collars as we checked all the hitches. This was the real thing, my first test in unknown country. I was determined to do my very best, to the limits of my ability, and earn Raefe's approval. My future could well depend upon his report.

In spite of the heavy load the team started at a fast pace, running over a mile on a well-packed trail. Raefe ran immediately behind the toboggan and could not have kept up with the dogs if he had not been holding onto the thick rope attached to the front of the outfit. It was also used as a rough-lock brake when going down a steep incline to prevent the load from running over the dogs. Wrapped around the toboggan, it had the same effect as a chain rough-lock on a wooden wagon wheel.

Although I started at a good pace on the smooth trail, it was not long before I lost sight of Raefe and the team as they turned north on the Sixtymile River. I didn't expect this and I plodded harder, encumbered in moccasins encased in mukluks. Running another mile I turned west and could see the team in the distance, about three miles ahead. I had no alternative but to keep running in their tracks and fortunately the trail continued solid under a fall of fresh snow, about three inches deep. After another five miles it turned north up Bedrock Creek but we continued up the Sixtymile, breaking new trail on the ice but still travelling in the valley.

We began to run into snow a foot deep and the team slowed to a walk, but I was still far behind. Eventually Raefe stopped them, which gave me time to catch up. He gave me a chance to get my breath back to normal as we sat silently on the loaded toboggan, then he lightened the moment with a bit of good-natured kidding.

"Did you wonder when you'd see me again?"

I nodded. He had also been running flat out, helped by the attached rope. But he was in better shape and had regained his wind.

"Break out the four-foot snowshoes," he said, "and try them on. Watch me retie the load, then try the shoes in deep snow."

We were both wearing two pairs of heavy wool socks, moccasins of caribou hide made by the Indians north of Dawson and mukluks that covered our feet with moosehide, the uppers of canvas reaching just below the knees.

I strapped on the awkward-looking contraptions

designed to prevent the wearer from sinking too far into deep snow. These were made with a bent willow frame, rounded in front and narrow behind, with a series of holes through which babiche, a thick thong of rawhide, is threaded, similar to a tennis racket.

Raefe watched in silence as I practised lifting each foot in turn, then cautiously taking a few short steps until I found out how to move without tripping. I was surprised at how quickly I adapted to the strange pace of stepping out with these wide, long additions to my feet. I went into deeper snow and marvelled at how they compressed the snow, allowing me to lift each foot in turn and waddle without losing my balance. Raefe watched with interest.

"Think you can handle them, and break trail ahead?"

"Feels fine, Raefe, but I don't think I could run with them."

"Just develop a steady pace. Follow the Sixtymile until you reach the next creek and turn up it until I signal."

I made fairly good progress until I reached the creek. Then I turned south and ran into deeper snow which slowed the pace. After a few miles Raefe signalled a halt. We removed half the load and cached it by securing it in canvas, well lashed. We were getting ready to climb the mountain ahead.

"Tich, get a good head start, for the dogs will pick up the pace with half a load until the climb gets steeper."

I struggled on up the creek and as it narrowed the exercise turned into hard work; the deeper snow was softer, making me lift my feet higher as the snowshoes sank into it. Raefe soon caught up with me.

"Leave the creek bed and make a trail through the bushes to the treeless area beyond."

I did so, finding that the ground rose sharply, but as I reached the treeless area, the snow was not so deep, having been blown away or compacted by the whistling wind. The higher I climbed, the more compacted was the snow, until there was just the imprint of the snowshoe frame and the pattern of the webbing to mark my trail for the dogs, now struggling as they leaned into their harness.

I was climbing more easily now and keeping well ahead, so I could look back occasionally and see other high mountains ranged in the distance. I could spot the team struggling up the steep grade a few inches at a time. Raefe was pulling on the rope, fighting to keep the toboggan from slewing around and sliding backward as they zig-zagged and tacked up the slope. As the day progressed I reached a height that permitted me to see the mountains to the south as well as those to the north. It was indeed awesome country in a landscape soundless except for the howl of the wind and the cold squeak of snowshoes protesting on the hard-packed trail. We could only guess at the temperature, but it is safe to say we weren't working up a sweat.

The ridge of the mountain range appeared to be running east and west. I kept shuffling west for several miles until I noticed Raefe signalling and I was glad to be able to rest my legs until they caught up. I figured we were near the Alaska border. Looking south, I could see a river in the valley and scrutinized its course for miles, certain that it would lead us to the White River. While the dogs were taking a well-earned rest, Raefe outlined the next move.

"We have to look for a 'pup' on the south side of
the range."

"What's a pup, Raefe?"

"It's a slight cut or notch in the range, leading off
the ridge, which would help to drain towards a creek,
which in turn would lead us to a river."

I got to my feet and started out ahead with additional admiration for a man who could read the landscape where I could see nothing. When he signalled me
to bear south off the ridge I could just detect, a hundred
yards ahead, a subtle change in the shape of the white
mass and soon picked up the route we needed to follow. I stopped, waiting for the senior man's confirma-
tion before proceeding, and then plunged down into
softer snow, not packed like the windward side.

Soon I was floundering in 18 inches of the white
stuff, and sinking deeper. It was a different kind of exercise from snowshoeing on the flat and I made slow,
cautious progress for five or six miles. Just as I was ready
to stop and wait for Raefe, I saw a log cabin and picked
up my pace, realizing that this was the place Raefe was
looking for. He had done his homework well and we were
safe after our first day, knowing we were on the right
creek and having travelled about 20 miles from the post
at Miller Creek.

There was no evidence that Harry Hanlon had used
this cabin. We had a date, for the calendar hanging on
the wall was marked October 25, 1927, four years before Hanlon had disappeared. While the exhausted dogs
lay in their harness, panting and recharging their bat-
teries, we unloaded the toboggan, placing everything inside the cabin. Then, without wasting time and what
light was left, we turned the team and retraced our steps

with the lightened toboggan, up and over the mountain. At the cache we picked up the rest of our supplies and struggled back with the second load. Reaching the cabin with our energy drained, we all relaxed, caught our wind and cooled off before making camp for the night.

There was nothing to indicate who had used the cabin since Hanlon may have passed through. It was a poor excuse for a shelter, without stove or bunks, the door and window missing and a dirt floor with drifts of snow. I stood by to help and my education continued as I watched Raefe tackle the problem of making this neglected ruin habitable.

First he chopped down a tree and with a six-foot snowshoe, he cleared snow away from an area in front of the cabin. Taking a few twiggy pieces that were coated with resin from the top of the tree, he crushed them in his hands. He rolled dry moss from the trunk around the twigs and applied a match. Then he fed tiny, thin branches to increase the weak flame, and as it grew stronger he added larger pieces of splinters until he had a fire that could take split logs.

At least I was able to look after the dogs, tying them to saplings close to the cabin. This was not easy as I had to handle each dog in snow several feet deep without the help of snowshoes in the restricted space. After feeding them their ration of fish, I watched Raefe chop off the lower six feet of the tree and with quick axe work flatten one side. He pushed this against the roaring fire with the flat side uppermost to serve as a stove top.

Not having eaten all day, except for the handful of raisins, we were famished, but we needed quick energy before tackling the rest of the chores. The frying pan scooped up enough snow to melt for a pot of tea which we consumed before the meal. With the frying pan balanced on the log and extended over the fire we put the beans in to thaw. As the liquid appeared Raefe added small pieces of fat pork and started soaking a couple of the hard-tack biscuits. We sat near the fire and ate our dinner. Then we made a second pot of tea, as we had perspired freely climbing the mountain, and had an additional treat with slices of bread and jam.

After washing up Raefe showed me how to make a bed on the dirt floor in the cabin. He collected an armful of small pine branches to serve as a mattress and I followed suit. Over this he placed his caribou skin and I used the canvas from the toboggan. Our sleeping bags went on top.

Outside, about eight feet from the fire, Raefe erected two wooden tripods with a sapling across the top between them. We removed our mukluks, moccasins and socks and hung them on this frame to dry overnight. Once the fire had thrown enough heat, we put on dry socks and moccasins, removed our parkas and placed them on top of our sleeping bags.

With all the chores completed we sat and stared at the fire, each with his own thoughts, until we were completely relaxed. Finally, on an unspoken signal, Raefe placed a couple of larger logs on the fire. We climbed into our bags and lay watching the fire through the open doorway until we slipped off into blissful sleep. The air conditioning was first class.

The sleeping bags were quite roomy for one person. Following the advice of my mentor I climbed in fully clothed, with my muskrat-fur cap on. Now it was time for acrobatics. With the bag fastened part way from the bottom, I wrestled out of the moccasins and placed them outside, near my head. I then fastened the bag all the way up until there was only a small opening for fresh air, which was so nippy I continued wearing the fur cap. It took a while before I could feel any warmth from my body and then it was time to start removing some clothing. Off came the windbreaker, then the heavy wool trousers and later, the heavy wool shirt. I stared at the dancing flames, fascinated, as my body warmed. Fatigue after the heavy exercise took over and quickly lulled me to sleep.

Wolves and Wickis

CHAPTER FIVE

*I*t was dark when we retired and it was still inky black when I surfaced from a deep sleep and opened my eyes to a moonless sky. I felt the prod from Raefe.

"Wakey, wakey, Watty," and then friendly advice. "Get yourself dressed inside the bag while I hustle the fire."

If it was difficult getting undressed that way, it was even harder doing it in reverse. Somehow I managed. The last item was the moccasins and they were right by my head. Struggling like a contortionist, in short order I had them on and laced. Raefe fed some split wood to the embers and the flames began to drive back the bitter cold as I danced around close by to retrieve my mukluks from the drying rack.

"Come on, Tich, let's get the blood circulating," he said, and started to jog back on the packed trail. I followed close behind as Raefe picked up the pace and we did a quarter of a mile before we turned and retraced our steps. Now we were warm enough for a quick wash with snow and a good rub down, and we were ready for the day.

It was my turn to cook and I served beans with pork, hard biscuits and a pot of coffee. When breakfast was over, the dishes washed and our gear packed, the sky had lightened and it was time to be off. Every day I was picking up something new, the right technique or established drill that had been tested to ensure safety and enable me to qualify as trail-wise.

I was beginning to feel we were shaping into a pretty good team. For instance, after the gruelling day crossing the mountain range twice, with half a load each time, I began to learn about sharing duties. The man who broke trail was expected, at the end of the day, to fall the tree necessary for warmth and meals before we were chilled. He was also expected to chop enough wood for the night and morning fire. The dog man had to unhitch the team, secure them safely and feed them.

Now it was my turn to drive and Raefe's to break trail. As no new snow had fallen during the night, he left wearing the four-foot snowshoes. I had to pack and lash the toboggan as I had been taught, make sure the fire was completely out, then harness the dogs. Ready for another day's work and nicely rested, the huskies were jumping up and down as they waved their bushy tails in jubilation. When I gave the command they leaned into their collars and the toboggan began to slip into life. They started at a fast pace for a mile, settling to a steady trot until gradually the load toned them down to a walking pace. From time to time I'd stop to give them a rest.

Two miles farther on, the little tributary joined a creek which we followed for three miles until Raefe's tracks led on to the Ladue River. I saw Raefe in the distance; the snow was deeper here but he was making good time. It was midday before the dogs caught up to him and earned their noon rest. We sat on the toboggan munching our raisins while Raefe explained what he wanted for a suitable site where no cabin was expected.

"We've got to find a grove of young saplings not too far from the river," he said.

"Not much choice along this stretch, Raefe."

"If the right spot shows up before our stopping time, I'll call a halt. Then I'll show you how to build a wicki."

We started out again, everyone in good fettle, and kept a steady pace with Raefe well in the lead and the dogs eager to catch up. Now and again we saw moose tracks crossing from one side of the river to the other, but no signs of fur-bearing animals. Missing in particular was any indication of the little snowshoe rabbit usually found in abundance in most areas of the Yukon. We plodded on in a grey, cold world, and darkness was catching up with us when Raefe finally signalled and turned to climb the river bank. The dogs followed his trail until we found him in a clearing among a small grove, with larger pine trees close by. I stood with the team until Raefe indicated where he would build the shelter, called a wickiup, or wicki for short. Then we got busy and cleared the snow away with the large snowshoes. As I was removing the dogs to tether and feed, Raefe was getting his fire started.

"Tie them as close to the fire as you can," he advised. "I've got a feeling this is wolf country."

I watched him set a thin sapling between the crotches of two trees, about six feet high; then he laid saplings against this to form a sloping roof. We covered this roof and both sides with branches. While I worked away at this Raefe got the usual meal ready and we topped it off with the last of the bread and jam.

"No more dessert this trip," said Raefe.

But we had an extra pot of tea and watched the flames as night and the creeping cold enfolded us. We were warm from our exercise and the meal helped maintain our body heat, but we could feel the cold nipping our cheeks on the side away from the fire. Then we finished the wicki, made our pine-bough beds, placed sleeping bags on caribou hide and canvas, and hung damp footwear from the cross-member, which was only six feet from the fire.

When I opened my eyes in the morning there were six inches of fresh snow on the ground. During the night Raefe had pushed an extra log on the fire with a long stick beside his bed, and with good embers for our breakfast fire we made an early start. It was my turn to break trail and I started well ahead with the smaller snowshoes. But by noon I was having trouble; I was sinking far enough into the softer snow to make a trench, causing snow to fall in on the snowshoes, and I had to work extra hard lifting each foot with its load before the next step.

I waited for Raefe to catch up, and while we took our "raisin rest" I changed to the six-foot snowshoes, which were wide and long enough to help widen the trail. It made for better going, but the best I could do was still only seven to ten miles a day, using more energy each step of the way.

It was also necessary for the man with the dogs to walk in front of the team, wearing the four-foot set, to help pack the trail for the load. I was finding my job such hard work I began looking forward to my turn with the team, when I could change to the shorter snowshoes. I did not realize at the time that there was no real advantage to either of the jobs.

As the afternoon ground on monotonously it started to snow and the air turned warmer. Six inches fell as we struggled, the big flakes sticking to my cheek or catching my eyelids, then melting. Not wearing a watch, I had no sense of time, and I kept looking back for Raefe's signal to call it a day. Finally I caught the message to stop, which meant to look for a site off the river that would meet Raefe's standards. It took me another two miles before I found one. The river was wider here, with many more game tracks, which I tried to read. Raefe explained later they indicated a fight between wolves and a doomed moose.

With deeper snow it took an extra effort to climb up the bank. We had to crab up sideways on the awkward shoes and I fell several times before I caught on. The dogs needed help as well to get the loaded toboggan off the river. I had no trouble dropping a tree, cutting it into suitable lengths and splitting it to make a fire while Raefe started building the wicki. I then helped lace the branches on roof and sides.

The closest we could tie the dogs was 50 feet from our wicki and we quickly fed them. Tired, they soon packed the snow under the shrubs, curled up with noses buried in tails and could not be seen. Neither did we linger by the fire this evening, for soon after dinner we climbed quickly into our bags and had no need for tranquillizers to put us to sleep.

During the night I thought I heard the dogs whimpering, but there was no other sound; they were out of sight and I drifted off. Seconds later Raefe climbed out of his sleeping bag in his underwear and threw a small piece of wood on the fire to get a quick blaze.

"There are wolves circling the dogs," he said. "You'd better get dressed."

We both got into our gear and I fed the fire while Raefe broke out the rifle and held it ready. As the fire crackled into life and penetrated the gloom, we could see the light reflecting in the yellow eyes of timber wolves. About five of them were pacing back and forth a short distance behind the dogs, who remained crouched. We stayed up the rest of the night and kept the fire burning brightly until at daybreak the menace faded away.

We lost little time breaking camp and leaving that sinister area. As it was Raefe's turn to break trail I was looking forward to an easier day, but I was in for another disappointment. As long as the trail was straight, the toboggan stayed on top and I had no trouble. But at the slightest bend the blasted thing slipped off the hard-packed snow into the deeper, softer stuff. I had to wrestle to keep it from tipping and steer it back on to the trail. Sometimes I would be breaking trail ahead of the team to improve Raefe's track when I'd glance back and see it not only off the trail but tilted over. Groaning at the energy I had used to get this far, I'd go back, drop into the deeper snow around the team, and manhandle the load back on the hard pack. After this had happened several times, I decided I would prefer to break trail ahead with the big shoes any time.

We fought on like this for another two days, making cold camp in wickis. There was nothing unusual to report in this vast and empty land. We were close to the mouth of the Ladue where it joins the White River. On the second night, as we sat silently before the fire, I began to realize that Raefe was as drained physically as I was. It was time to assess the situation. I stared at the flames and thought of Harry Hanlon, wondering if he had travelled this far and what could have happened. Raefe snapped me out of my reverie.

"Tomorrow we head back for Miller Creek."

"Are you convinced Hanlon never came this way?"

Raefe took his time before replying.

"No trapper with Harry's experience would spend time building a wicki, let alone a cabin, where there's no sign of game."

"I thought we had to reach the headwaters of the White."

"We stop at the closest point to the Alaska border."

Raefe must have read my thoughts, or felt the disappointment in my mood after the struggle to get here.

"Look," he added, "there's no sign of the snowshoe rabbit, and the lack of small game accounts for the absence of lynx. Hanlon wouldn't waste a day in this country."

We turned in, deciding to make an early start at daybreak, and found it a lot easier going back. No one had to break trail, for the snow had been well packed and the dogs were eager to travel. The load was lighter, with more than half the dog food depleted and only a small amount of the 90 pounds of beans we had started with. The man handling the dogs was able to hang onto the rope, which made running easier, and the other could jog without snowshoes, catching up easily when the team stopped to rest. With a lighter load and a fast track, we made good time.

As we neared the mountain range and our most critical test, we were relieved to find the snow had been compacted by strong winds. But we also had to change from moccasins and mukluks to waterproof boots because we ran into wet areas caused by underground warm springs. Then as we climbed to higher elevations we had to travel over areas covered with glacial ice. The dogs began to have trouble, slipping and sliding while struggling up the steeper grades. We tried to help, pushing from behind and pulling on the rope.

One dog wrenched a shoulder and had to be taken out to follow. Raefe and I then put ice creepers on our boots for better purchase. With one pulling on the rope ahead and the other pushing, we were able to assist the dogs over the glacier and reach the top of the range at about 5,000 feet, where it was more level. But here we found another obstacle. Since we had passed that way, very strong winds had struck, whipping the compacted snow away, and now sharp, pointed rocks scarred the toboggan and slowed our progress.

Eventually we reached the point where we had to start our descent to the Sixtymile valley. Though we could not see our destination, just knowing it was not far away lifted our spirits. We managed to descend to a reasonable grade on hard, compacted, but slippery snow. We made a couple of miles helping the dogs control the toboggan, manually braking and steering, until the slope became too steep and Raefe called a halt. He fashioned a rough-lock around the load and under the toboggan to help us keep it from running over the dogs. Then he told me to ride on the load to keep it balanced and to use my feet as a brake, as well as to guide the toboggan away from the dogs.

We managed another two miles, carefully and slowly, until we reached an exceedingly steep area and everyone stopped by common consent, the team needing a breather. We had to consider this obstacle. Raefe stood for longer than usual without comment, scanning the landscape. Then he broke the silence.

"Tich, we've got a problem that could mean trouble. The snow is hard as ice and that's why we're sliding all over the place."

"I can see that, but how are we going to get down?"

"I want you to sit farther back and I'll stand on the end of the toboggan. Our weight should make the rope rough-lock bite into the snow."

When the toboggan started to move, the dogs kept ahead as we slanted across the slope. The rough-lock was working, preventing the load from running over them, and we began to make better progress. From time to time I could not prevent the toboggan from slipping sideways, but when the rough-lock bit into a softer spot control returned. Raefe was tense as he guided the team away from dangerous areas, looking for patches where the snow was not hard and shiny. Our descent was often checked by an occasional rise which we climbed before the next grade.

We topped one rise and paused as we studied a longer, steeper slope presenting a more formidable obstacle. I stared in awe and turned to Raefe, who nodded and started the dogs moving. In spite of our best efforts, the toboggan picked up momentum and the dogs increased their pace to keep ahead. We were just managing to get away with it when the toboggan hit a snow-covered rock and whipped sideways with such force that Raefe and I parted company and went into orbit.

I found myself sliding down the mountain on my back, out of control and gaining speed until I reached the timber-line. My progress slowed when I started bouncing off stunted trees. Then I crashed into a taller stand at the lower level and came to a wrenching halt. I got to my feet slowly, relieved to find there were no broken bones. I took a few steps and there were no sprains, only a sore shoulder. Then I looked for Raefe and found him on his feet, about 50 yards away among a group of small trees. He was looking for the dogs.

By the time I reached him he had spotted the team, still attached to the toboggan, some distance farther down. We hurried to reach them before they attempted to move, if they were able. Raefe got the dogs straightened out, ran his hands carefully over each one until he was satisfied there were no serious injuries, checked the toboggan and load, then turned to me with a small grin.

"Lady Luck was riding with us, Tich. When I got tossed I landed on my back. Knocked the wind out of me and when I came to I was tumbling into the trees. Thank God the dogs are okay."

Had the toboggan hit a dog or one of us at that speed, it could have been a different story. In that un-forgiving terrain and climate, without today's means of communication, a simple mistake could be curtains. We began to realize how exceedingly lucky we had been.

After we got ourselves sorted out and calmed down, we followed the tree line until we found softer snow and a gentler slope, and were able to hold the toboggan back more easily. But we still proceeded cautiously, seeking ahead for tell-tale signs of hidden rocks. Eventually we found our original trail. It was filled with snow but we were able to follow it to the Sixtymile River without having to use snowshoes. Then the pace picked up. It was a great feeling, getting off that mountain range and knowing nothing could stop us now. Threats and danger behind, with a lighter load, we took turns riding or running behind and holding onto the rope. The dogs, sensing they were closing in on the haven at Miller Creek, raised their bushy tails and waved them jauntily. With their amazing recuperative powers, they did not look or act like animals that had worked extremely hard for nine days.

We pressed on, tired but jubilant, until in the gathering dark we reached the police building at Miller. Raefe, without a word, disappeared indoors while I slowly unharnessed the dogs, fastened each to his kennel and quickly got their rations to them. With my remaining strength I unloaded the toboggan. Then I noticed smoke curling from the chimney. Good old Raefe had it organized. There would be hot water and food for more civilized comfort. I picked up my sleeping bag and made my weary way towards the light.

After nine days of beans, fat pork and hardtack, the delicious smell of Raefe's cooking was something I will never forget. He had moose steaks sizzling in his big frying pan, a pot full of dehydrated potatoes looking creamy, for he had added canned milk, and a tin of canned corn. We topped it off with biscuits and a tin of plums, which turned it into a royal feast. After the gruelling hazards of a long day, I doubt if our table manners were very regal. I did not realize just how tired I was until we were working on the second pot of tea after dinner. An overwhelming urge to curl up anywhere soft and warm was broken by the disciplined voice of Raefe, the Corporal.

"There's enough hot water in the copper boiler for our bath."

"Jeez, Raefe, couldn't it wait?"

"And we'll heat more water for the dishes," he said.

I got the tub off the nail behind the stove and brought in more wood. Raefe, undressed and ready, was not able to stretch out in the small, round tub and lost no time lathering his body head to toe and washing it off. The water was still quite warm when I followed, and I began to glow with a beautiful sensation. I did not feel completely clean, however, as I was unaccustomed to not shaving each day. Nine days of stubble did not sit well.

With the chores finished, I was pleased to hear Raefe say he was turning in. He took the single cot and I spread my sleeping bag on the kitchen floor, using Raefe's caribou-skin and sleeping bag for a mattress. Though I slept like a babe, when I crawled out in the morning I was as stiff as a board. I actually missed those springy pine boughs on the trail!

Although it appeared to be daylight, the sky was leaden. I heard Raefe get up, light the coal-oil lamp and tend the stove and air-tight heater. I had an easy morning after feeding the dogs and ourselves. While Raefe typed his report and completed his diary, I had a chance to review the experience. I had finished my first serious patrol, survived the hardships and the tests of endurance, and had thoroughly enjoyed the challenge. But never again would I be satisfied with ordinary, routine police work around headquarters. Raefe interrupted my thoughts.

"By the look of the sky I think we're going to get more snow. When I finish the report we'll have a bite and start for Dawson."

"What can I do?"

"Pack enough fish and grub for four days. We may have to snowshoe most of the way."

"I hate to go back to barracks, Corp."

I finished loading everything we would need for a short run, lashed the load and hooked up the team. Raefe checked it over, pulling on the hitches.

"Pretty good. Has to be tight. With a light load one of us can ride."

We were on our way, shooting past the trapper's cabin at the mouth of Miller Creek. The dogs ran for another three miles before they settled down. Again I wondered if these animals could sense they were finally going home. As we turned up California Creek from the Sixtymile River I noticed the sky brightening, but later it darkened again, followed by snowflakes drifting by. The stuff came down more heavily until I had the sensation we were pushing through a white wall. I found it hard to define trees in the distance and with no horizon began to stumble a bit. It was almost a whiteout. Large flakes would stick to my face, and then melt. Fortunately it was not cold.

The next cabin we reached was similar to the ones on Swede and California. I did not have to be told what to do. The dogs were soon cared for and we were sitting on the bunks eating a light meal. During the day six inches of snow had fallen and it was still snowing when we retired. In the morning we faced 18 inches of fresh snow and I was glad we had cut and stacked our wood supply the night before. Raefe lost no time getting us away.

"You'll have to start with the short shoes until we get part way down the creek."

"Okay-dokey, then what?"

"We'll probably run into water on top of the ice. It overflows when the weather is mild."

"I'll watch for it," I replied.

"The overflow pushes snow ahead on the ice and forms a dam between the walls of the creek. Water backs up and then sweeps it away."

"Will this cost us another day?"

"Depends. We could stop at the last cabin before the Yukon, or we could press on. What's your choice?"

I was just as eager to reach Dawson as the dogs, but with mixed feelings. The thought of returning as an experienced, trail-wise northern man with some anecdotes and a line to shoot was tempting. But I did not relish the thought of returning to the barracks routine. However, I was beginning to understand the moods and wishes of Corporal Raefe Douthwaite.

"If you want to carry on to Dawson, I'm game."

"Right. We'll see how we get along on Swede Creek."

I started out with the shorter snowshoes, but put them back on the toboggan when we reached the overflow. We came to places where the water was nearly a foot deep until the dam of wet snow broke free. The water then rushed over the ice towards the Yukon River, sweeping snow ahead towards the next dam. The grade on Swede Creek steepened so we picked up time on the slippery ice.

When we reached the Yukon, fortune was riding with

us. The overnight snow, which had filled the trail, had been packed smooth by another team heading for Dawson. We made great time, with running conditions nearly perfect, and the dogs increased their eager pace as the miles slipped by. When we reached Dawson, in the early afternoon, Raefe let me handle the team, and as we swept into the compound I probably exhibited a bit more flourish than was strictly necessary.

It was gratifying to have an audience of chaps off duty as we pulled up at the rear of the building, and many hands helped to unload. Then I took the team to the kennels. After feeding the dogs and putting the equipment in storage, I entered the barracks, where I found my kit on my bed, and I began to peel off. Raefe had not wasted time. He was soaking in the big bath where he could stretch out. I planned to be next.

After a wonderful soak, and dressed in a clean uniform, I bumped into Sergeant Cronkhite.

"I hear you had a good trip, Watson, but the search was without result."

"That's right, Sergeant."

He rattled off questions, probing for details of the patrol and my own reaction to events as if he was scoring my performance. I had to be careful, precise in my statements, and again I realized how much I had been taught by and had absorbed from Raefe's thorough coaching.

The final report stated that a relentless search for Harry Hanlon had been made over several years to establish whether or not he had met with an acccident or foul play. No trace of the man was found. The investigation remained "Unconcluded," in police terms, with the hope that eventually some evidence would surface to establish why he disappeared suddenly, without a trace.

His cabins, trapping equipment and registered trap lines were sold to a couple of young men by the public administrator after the report had been submitted. They later became involved in a dispute over ownership of one of the cabins, and once again I would become involved in the estate and mystery of Harry Hanlon.

Detachment Takeover

CHAPTER SIX

As Sergeant Cronkhite was in charge of Town Station, I asked him when I should report for duty.

"I suggest you wait until things are sorted out. Sergeant major will want to see you before you return to me."

I joined the others off duty and began to indulge myself in describing details of obstacles, climbs, tumbles, and wolves, and how we managed to overcome the problems. When Raefe appeared with a look of amusement, I suddenly became a bit more modest. The boys drifted away and the corporal took a chair.

"Glad to be back in your old bed?"

"Well, sort of, but it feels awful soft."

He laughed. "From now on you'll get used to anything."

I went to the sergeant major's office for permission to slip into town in civvies to do some shopping.

"You can take the rest of the day off after the officer commanding has seen you."

I followed the senior non-commissioned officer down the hall to the command post of the Yukon. He knocked and walked in. I followed.

"Constable Watson, sir." He quietly departed, closing the door, and I stood alone in front of the famous Superintendent Tommy Caulkin. He looked at me searchingly.

"Watson, I would like to know if you feel ready to handle a detachment by yourself."

Stunned by the question, for which I was not prepared, I began to flounder for a sentence, a qualifying statement. Then I remembered Raefe on the trail and how he would manage to make a decision.

"Yes, sir." No ifs or buts or let me try it. I waited.

"Right. That's what I wanted to hear. The sergeant major will arrange for you to take over Miller Creek from Corporal Douthwaite."

Surprised, nervously excited, I tried to remain calm as I thanked him. He rose from his chair, came round the desk, grabbed my hand and shook it.

"Good luck, Watson. Take care. Douthwaite says you're ready."

I thanked him again and floated down the hall. I'd be on my own, independent, free of the barracks routine. Sergeant Major Davies treated me with more ease, as if I had suddenly grown up. I was to have a couple of days free of duty to get ready. Then I was to return to Miller Creek with Raefe to take over officially.

The day we were to leave Dawson for the take-over of Miller Creek detachment, I was still the novice. Raefe, as senior man, made the decisions until he had signed over his territory to me. With responsibility deferred, I enjoyed another breakfast of bacon and sourdough hotcakes and helped load our gear in the carryall in a carefree spirit. But when it came time to harness up, I was back in school, for we were replacing the veteran Dawson dog team with the five youngsters assigned to Miller Creek that Raefe had been training. I stood by, waiting for instructions.

"These dogs are not fully trained so I want you to notice my style of drill. Always remember they're green, and they don't understand all the usual commands."

He filled me in on their background and temperament. They had been supplied to the force by a breeder near Dawson named Percy DeWolfe. Four of the malemutes had a quarter wolf strain and one was half wolf. They were the offspring of domestic female dogs crossed with male timber wolves. Raefe had named four of them after creeks and rivers.

The leader was "Miller," the number two "Glacier," next was "Ladue" and the wilder one, which he called "Wolf," was placed in front of the wheel dog, the largest and strongest in the team. His name was "Bedrock," which suited him perfectly, and he was fastened independently so the driver could "Gee" or "Haw" him right or left to change direction in a hurry.

I watched and noted how Raefe handled each animal. He would ruffle the hair on their heads and make soothing sounds as he led them out in turn to be hitched to the sleigh. He took his time and continued talking to them as he placed their legs inside the traces, and when he had a good hold on the handlebars he rolled out his first command.

"Easy, easy . . . easy . . . . Aaaalright."

By the second "Easy" the dogs were prancing, tails up and waving, shoulders into their collars, and when they heard "Aaaalright," they leapt forward in unison and were away at high speed. Raefe kept his balance with one foot on a runner and the other on the brake. Of course I had jumped aboard on his first signal and we did an exhilarating fast clip for about two miles before the youngsters eased into a loping trot.

When we reached the mouth of Swede Creek, Raefe called a halt. The dogs were panting, their dripping tongues extended.

"We'll have to go easy until they harden up," he said, "but travel conditions are ideal after two days of 40 degrees of frost. New ice powdered with light snow couldn't be better."

When we started out again the team settled down quickly to a steady trot that slowed to a walk as we climbed to higher ground. I ran behind until we reached the first cabin, where the dogs rested while we munched our ration of raisins. Then we continued to the cabin at the divide on Fish Creek, where Raefe decided the youngsters had expended enough energy without breaking their spirit and we would spend the night.

Each of us followed the procedure we had established on the missing-trapper patrol and in no time we were comfortably enjoying a meal prepared by Raefe; a few extra dainties from town included canned fruit and bakery buns.

Raefe had us up early in the morning and he watched and coached while I tried my hand with the new team

I used the same sounds and words, making first contact with a few strokes on each head. We reached the Miller Creek quarters late in the afternoon and Raefe began at once to point out items I'd be responsible for. In addition to dog food, coal-oil, harness and tools, there were three pairs of snowshoes, simple furniture, a stove, a heater, a 30-30 calibre rifle, 50 cartridges and 20 pairs of caribou booties for the dogs to wear in conditions of crystallized ice or snow. I also had to sign for a typewriter, ledger, daily diary and all the law books, federal and territorial. Then for two days I worked with the green team while Raefe took me around the district to visit key people on Glacier, Miller and Bedrock creeks. On the Sixtymile River we called at the Holbrook Dredging Company, where I met the brothers Frank and Ed Holbrook and Ed's son, Bud.

At these casual stops Raefe taught me the trick of the quiet command. "Down . . . down," he would say, sometimes with a hand signal, and to my amazement it worked. They would lie right down, keeping their eyes on him. Raefe had improved on the usual drill of roping the sleigh or toboggan to a tree or building. It took me a while to accept that mutual trust existed between animal and man, for this was not an accepted practice.

When Raefe was satisfied and I had signed the completed forms, I was officially in charge and responsible for the post. All I had to do was take the corporal back to Dawson, and we made an uneventful trip with a light load over a well-packed trail. I drew into the compound with a self-satisfied flourish and Raefe disappeared. With critical eyes watching, I ordered the team "Down" and they dropped in their tracks. I hesitated about leaving them unattended, but took a chance and followed Raefe.

I dumped my load and hurried back to a wonderful sight. The dogs had not moved.

I drove the outfit to the kennels, and fed and fussed with the team, proud they were giving me their loyalty. They were resting comfortably when Raefe turned up, and I could guess why. I disappeared into the store room with the equipment while he spent some time alone with each dog. As we walked back to barracks, he put his arm over my shoulder.

"Well, buddy, you're on your own now. Best luck."

"Raefe, you've been a damn fine, patient teacher. I'll think of you often out in those hills, working with your dogs."

I went off to pack my personal effects and left Dawson early the following morning. My only disappointment was that Raefe didn't show up to watch us leave. It wasn't until years later that I would understand, when it was my turn to hand over these lovely animals to my successor. The lead dog had saved my life on one occasion, and I too failed to show up when they trotted out of my control.

I started out as though I had been mushing dogs for years, but in the first hours of this solo journey I began to ponder my responsibilities. Why hadn't I asked more questions? What should I do if I caught someone smuggling, or hunting without a license? No one had really briefed me on patrol duties or how to cope with unpredictable situations. The post did not have a lockup and the nearest magistrate was at Dawson. I was facing the uncertainty every young policeman finds himself in, alone in a district with scattered strangers curious to watch, and ready to criticize, every move.

Now I represented the government and the laws of

the territory, which included criminal code, federal statutes, customs, immigration, taxes, even migratory birds. I did not realize at the time that I would have to learn the philosophy of keeping the peace in the Yukon, that it was still very much the frontier, different from any other part of Canada. I was about to enter a lifestyle and gain experience which, looking back down the years, would help me throughout my life.

Arriving at the post, my thoughts turned domestic. After settling the dogs, I lit the heater, which took the chill off the well-constructed log building. Then I packed away the provisions that Raefe had suggested I purchase. These included powdered milk, rice, shredded dehydrated potatoes, dried apricots, raisins, prunes, apples and the old stand-by, beans. In addition to ten pounds of hard-tack biscuits, I had included a tin of jam, which Raefe had mentioned might be handy for unexpected company.

The mining company near by employed a number of single men and ran a cook-house which Raefe had used for convenience. Ray Miller, the manager, and his son, Gordie, who also operated the post office, invited me to eat at their mess hall. I took advantage the first day and found a warm welcome from the hardworking miners, and the food was a distinct improvement over the grub at Dawson. I hung around for half an hour getting to know the crew before walking back to the detachment.

After lighting the lamp, I pulled the office chair to the table and tried to read a book, my first night alone. The combination of warm cabin and full tummy blurred the printed page and I began to nod. I banked the heater and crawled into bed. It had been a full day.

It was dark when I woke and the cabin had cooled off. I stoked the heater, found it was only five o'clock and climbed back into bed. I dozed until 6:30 which gave me half an hour to wash, dress and jog to breakfast. Back at the office, I looked at the blank page of the diary and wondered what I should do first. My previous experience on saddle-horse patrols had taught me that Yukoners were generally pleased when I called and took an interest in their progress. This would be a good way to start.

The Millers had given me the names and locations of miners and prospectors on Glacier and Bedrock Creeks. There was just one man working alone near the head of Miller Creek and I decided he might welcome a visit. I laced on the four-foot snowshoes and plodded up Miller. There I found an elderly man named Miller, who was somewhat surprised to see me. He wasn't used to visitors and left me with the impression that he did not want his solitude disturbed too often. He was not related to the other Millers. It was a short visit and I decided to leave him alone for six months. On my next visit he was working his claim and I pitched in. We got to know each other better, and after that I visited him once a month.

It was three miles from the detachment to the Holbrook Dredging Company, and I made regular calls there to pick up information and advice from Ed. One day he sent a man for me, and it must have been urgent, for the guy stood in the doorway, panting, before he exploded.

"Ed's afraid he won't make it."

"Won't make what?" I demanded.

"All the way to Dawson. He's never been over the

winter trail . . . never used snowshoes . . . he'll never make it.''

''Who're you talking about?''

''Guy Gertsen . . . lives in a cabin near the upper road . . . a bad tooth is driving him crazy.''

''Why can't Ed take him to Dawson?''

''Dog team's there now. Ed doesn't know when it'll be back.''

It looked as though I would have to make the run, and we walked towards the camp, parting company at the fork leading to the Gertsen cabin.

''Tell Mr. Holbrook I'll look after it,'' I said.

It was a steep climb for a quarter of a mile, but well packed, as Gertsen used it daily. At the cabin I knocked and entered to face a well-built young man, about 25 years old, who stood without a word. One side of his face was badly swollen. I held out my hand.

''I'm Constable Watson. Are you Gertsen?''

He nodded and pointed to a young lady.

''My wife, Olga,'' he mumbled.

She was putting a cute little girl of two years to bed.

''I'm sorry, Mrs. Gertsen, for barging in when you're trying to get the child to sleep. Heard your husband was going to Dawson alone with a bad tooth.''

''Yes,'' she replied. ''Had it three weeks. Can't stand the pain any longer.''

I took a chair and looked around. The cabin was small, one room crowded with two single cots, the baby's crib, two chairs and a table. A pail of water was sitting on a block of wood beside the stove and there was little room for anything else. Near the door was a loaded pack and a pair of snowshoes. I took out my notebook and made some doodles after his name while I tried to think. Although I had first-aid training, dentistry was not included. In my medical supplies there was some rubbery substance which could pack a cavity and give some relief. I told Gertsen about it.

"Mind if I look at your teeth?"

He nodded and I sat him in a chair with the light from the Coleman lantern full on his face. I washed my hands, peered at a mouth full of teeth, inserted a finger and gently ran it along the gums. He winced when I touched close to a large molar. I washed and dried my hands again and thought about the long journey to Dawson. Snow conditions meant someone would have to break trail ahead of the dogs, and it would take three days at least to cover the 80 miles.

"If Holbrook has forceps, I'm ready to try and extract it."

"No good," said Olga. "Ole Johansen tried."

"If I can't, then I'll take you to Dawson."

Gertsen jumped up, grabbed his fur cap and coat without a word and left the cabin. In no time he was back, out of breath, with a case of evil-looking instruments. I had him lie down and gave him a couple of aspirins while I washed again. Then, to give them more confidence than I felt, I took some time looking over the selection and picked up an ugly pair of forceps with a curved head shaped like a claw hammer.

The patient was now back in the chair by the light, gripping it firmly, his head back and body rigid. He let me grasp the offending molar with a veritable death grip. I exerted steady pressure, using the adjoining tooth as a fulcrum. There wasn't a sound, except for a deep moan from the patient, and I hung on for dear life. Suddenly

I lost my balance and thought the damn forceps had slipped off the tooth.

Gertsen's arms were around me and I thought he was about to attack. I whirled to face him and there was a big grin.

"It's out, it's out," he mumbled.

I looked at the forceps in my white-knuckled hand and there was the four-pronged brute in the instrument's ugly jaws. The relief was general, as the poor man's suffering was over and my dogs would not have to make a tough journey.

Mrs. Gertsen ran to her husband and hugged and kissed him. She grasped my hands and her voice choked as she said, "I can't believe it."

She was so excited she had trouble finding the coffee pot, and while the patient was tending to his bleeding cavity, stuffing a dressing of cotton in the empty socket, Olga took his things out of the pack and put them away. They wouldn't be needed now. He was a tough young man. He moved easily as he placed the chairs for his wife and guest and removed the water pail from the block of wood, which he rolled to the table for his seat.

Olga served the coffee and also placed slices of home-made bread on the table with butter and jam. I watched Guy lift his cup to his lips, then put it down again. His mouth was obviously too tender. He caught me looking at him and said with a smile, "I'll have to cool it a bit more."

He was able to talk more easily now, and it turned into a visit where we learned about each other. Olga started to break the ice.

"My mother is now married to Joe Stingle and they

live in Dawson. He used to cook for the police. Do you know Joe?''

"I met him briefly,'' I replied.

"They're talking of moving to Bedrock to prospect.''

"That's part of my territory. I'll look out for them.''

I gave the folks a summary of my background and learned the Gertsens were of Danish descent and had moved from the prairies. I had now made new friends, so important to a policeman alone. In future, when I patrolled along the upper road, I would check the post office at Miller Creek. If there was anything for the Gertsens I would drop it off.

I tried to be friendly with everyone, but not too close. I did not make a practice of visiting any one particular family because it could tempt me to take sides in any dispute. And I never tried practising dentistry again.

When it was time to hang popular local and convicted murderer Barney West, a scaffold had to be built. Here, special constable Alec Craig helps with construction.

Sergeant Bert Johns with ''Mr. Ellis''—Canada's hangman, 1932.

The detachment at Miller Creek. With both a wood cookstove and a wood heater, it was luxurious compared to most trail cabins.

Better than a bear hug. Sled dog Gufus at play with Corporal Douthwaite, Miller Creek.

On patrol with the dog team. Here, the author and team pose beside moose tracks.

Douthwaite demonstrates how to walk in snowshoes. . .and what happens if you don't.

When no cabin was available, the author and Douthwaite constructed a wicki (background) from saplings and branches. In the foreground are a six-foot snowshoe, a four-foot snowshoe, and a 30-30 rifle.

Climbing Snag Mountain with half a load.

Trapper Wagner's cabin and fur storage house (right background) where the author bought a bearskin for five dollars.

Spring breakup, 1933. The roar of the Yukon River in flood was heard after the ice had erupted, cracking and grinding and throwing chunks into the air.

An alternate mode of travel: lining boats up the Fortymile River en route to Alaska.

The canyon at Fortymile River.

Constable Reg Sheppard and telegraph linesman Bunny Lilievre at the linesman's cabin at Ogilvie on the Yukon River, after a special patrol to solve a dispute at White River.

Reg Sheppard, chosen for his stamina and courage to accompany the author on the New Year's Eve patrol to White River.

Walter King, a Dawson character loved by all the people as well as by all the dogs in town, posing here with a four-footed friend.

Saddle horse patrol, Dawson, April 1933.

Camping overnight on the search for prospector Theodore Tomsk.

Louie Lyckens with a timber wolf pup he and his brother raised.

The author on saddle horse patrol at Gold Creek.

The author (front) and Ole Medby on a modified sleigh.
Note that in the top photo, the dogs, still fresh, have
their tails up and wagging. Below, tired after a run to
Dawson, their tails are down.

The author (right) with prospector Theodore Tomsk.

Learning
Detachment Work

CHAPTER SEVEN

*L*ong before the gold rush and the mad stampede of adventurers from all over the world, explorers and trappers had been following trails through the mountains from Alaska to the junction of the Klondike and Yukon rivers. This mountain range divides the watersheds of the Fortymile and Sixtymile rivers, both of which join the mighty Yukon. The early adventurers walked with packs on their backs, then used dogs to pack or pull a toboggan. Some later had the luxury of a pack horse when the trail was open, generally four months of the year, June to September.

Gradually, as more traffic was generated between Alaska and the Yukon, it was necessary to widen the trail to allow horse-drawn wagons to carry freight between the larger settlements. Ed Holbrook, who leased a gold dredge from Billy Williams, used a section of this road extensively in summer and eventually brought in a small tractor to pull a wagon. From Fairbanks, Anchorage and Chicken Creek in Alaska, goods and supplies moved back and forth to Dawson, from where they would be carried by water. The closest point in Alaska to Dawson was the settlement of Jack Wade Creek.

After the first fall of snow a winter trail had to be made, using the creeks flowing into the Yukon, by dog team. Either the RCMP or Holbrook's outfit would make the first run, but sometimes the mail carrier from Dawson would be the first through to Sixtymile, following what was called the "Ridge Road." Today it is known internationally as the "Top Of The World Highway," a veritable mecca for tourists.

This winter trail would be used until excessive snow-fall made it impassable. Then a new winter route would be established from Sixtymile up California Creek, over a divide into a small creek leading to Swede Creek, then on to the Yukon River leading to Dawson. It would be in constant use until the break-up of ice on the Yukon in spring. Most of the freight from Alaska was hauled in winter following the Fortymile River via Jack Wade Creek. The importer could report to the police at Fortymile instead of going all the way to the collector of customs at Dawson, saving expense and time. I also acted as customs officer at Sixtymile.

Settlers in these areas near the international boundary were cut off from Dawson for uncertain weeks in spring and fall when heavy ice was running. In emergencies, in the days before telephones, radio, vehicles or aircraft, they looked to the RCMP for assistance.

Police in single detachments had to be dedicated and very straight to have any effect on the prevention of crime. The Sixtymile district had been producing gold continuously since long before the big strike near Dawson and today is reputed to be producing more than ever with modern methods. Yet during all this time not a single theft of gold has been reported.

The policeman in an isolated post had many caps to wear and his success depended upon gaining and holding the respect of the small communities. In addition to upholding Canadian law, he was responsible for issuing licenses and could take oaths and affidavits. He was expected to handle disputes, without court hearings, to the satisfaction of all parties. Sometimes, in the absence of a clergyman, he would officiate at burials. Having to substitute for doctor or dentist was not uncommon, but the man on detachment would consider getting the patient to the doctor a priority.

I was kept busy year round with these concerns, but I also had enough domestic duties to keep me out of mischief. In addition to feeding and watering the team, I had to clean the kennels and keep the dogs in shape in summer as well as winter. In the absence of sledding and snow, I would occasionally hitch them to a light log to pull a sufficient distance to keep up their muscle tone and general health. When I was away on foot patrols I had to arrange for someone to look after them.

I tried to visit every soul in my district several times a year and keep tabs on any need. I found miners on the creeks near the headwaters of the Sixtymile, at Glacier, All Gold, Big Gold and Miller. If someone's mail was held longer than normal, I would act as postman. Often this surprised people who lived in remote places and collected their mail once or twice a year. They were used to privation and loneliness, sending an order to Dawson by a passing stranger, picking up their supplies at a pre-arranged cache. I soon realized how very important these patrols were when I was first posted to Miller Creek.

Mushing down the Sixtymile in my first winter, I came upon a good-sized cabin in a remote spot, climbed the bank of the river, pulled up and went through the drill of patting each dog on the head and ordering them "Down." Waiting for them to settle quietly, I felt an eerie sensation when I looked around. The place was as quiet as a graveyard, no smoke or sign of life. I broke the silence with a hulloo and the team looked up, startled.

Then an old collie came shuffling around from behind the cabin, his joints stiff, and snuffled up to me. Just when I was trying to figure that one out, the dog wagged his tail and looked up. I turned and watched a character climbing down from a large pine. As he stepped to the ground I noticed the branches had been trimmed to give him a ladder to the top. It gave him a neat look-out covering the trail in both directions and I guess it was his own method of security.

He approached with a smile and a warm welcome. Short and stocky, in his forties I guessed, he was from the old country, a well-read, fairly well-educated Englishman who had been living alone long enough to be starved for company and news of the outside. I was invited into his pleasant cabin, where he soon had a fire going and the coffee pot busy. He set out some fine pottery instead of the usual enamel mugs and we sat in comfortable chairs. I could sense he was anxious to start a conversation, but good manners prevailed until I was settled and had consumed some of his good brew.

"You surprised me, coming out of the tree," I exclaimed.

"My dog told me a stranger, or large animal, was approaching, so I went up for a look."

"Were you expecting trouble?"

"Not really, but when you're alone, it's best to take care."

"With that dog, nothing's going to jump you."

"That's right. Are you looking for someone?"

"This is just a routine patrol to find who's living where and if they have any problems."

"No complaints here. I've got a snug cabin, enough to eat and a good trap-line. But I sure miss having someone to talk to besides this old dog."

The black-and-white collie looked up and thumped his tail. I learned he was trained to hide and was not to appear until his master started climbing down. Then my host pumped me for news and though I didn't know what was going on outside any more than he did, I had lots of items of local interest. I think his name was Wagner and it was obvious he was desperately lonely, starved for the sound of another human voice. He made me more than just welcome. He took care of the dogs and persuaded me to stay overnight. I revelled in more comfort and companionship than I was used to.

He talked his head off, describing his background and interests. Just as I started to doze he'd think of another question, and off we'd go again. I had to relate my experiences and travels in Canada, my initiation to the Yukon, the changes taking place in Dawson and the activities of his distant neighbours. I am sure he was still droning on as I finally fell into a deep sleep.

At breakfast he pleaded with me to stay a second night. I had to tell him that would be unusual practice and hard to explain in my patrol diary. He used various means to delay my departure, bringing out his books and family photographs, then provided another excellent meal at noon. Just as I got ready to depart he said that he had something interesting to show me.

We walked through the snow on a beaten path to another log building, about 15 by 18 feet, hidden in the trees. He unlocked and threw open the door and motioned me inside. I stood and stared, flabbergasted, at the sight of furs, everything the country produced, sorted and stacked rafter-high. I could scarcely believe one person could have so many rich furs at one time. He must have had all his wealth tied up in that remote cabin.

"Why don't you sell them?" I had to ask.

"I'm waiting for the prices to rise. I sell a few, just enough to keep me supplied with necessities."

I knew he would only require staples, for he could supply his own fresh meat whenever he needed, and a hole in the permafrost would keep it refrigerated. As he went through the piles of fur, turning them over to show how well the skins had been cleaned and treated, I could tell he was proud of their quality. He displayed various species so I could run my hands through the silky hairs and when he had me interested, made a final effort.

"Pick yourself a fur," he said, "and spend one more night."

I weighed the temptation, but remembered the cardinal rule. Never let word get out that you are a receiver, just riding the grub line for handouts. I thanked him but demurred and stopped stroking the sensual skins. As I turned to leave I noticed a young black bear skin which shone like silk in the light from the open door. "Tell you what," I said. "I need a rug and I'll buy that bearskin. How much do you want?"

"That little thing? I've got better big ones."

"I just want a small one to put my feet on when I get out of bed."

"Five dollars," he said without hesitation.

I stayed the second night.

So far, during my time in the Yukon, I had made patrols on horseback and on foot, in boats and by dog team. I thought I had moved about the country by every primitive means I could find, even hitching rides on wagons, sleighs and tractors, but in my early days at Miller Creek I discovered other methods.

It came about when Ed Holbrook, manager of the dredging company at Sixtymile, posed a problem. Whenever they had a large shipment of gold for Dawson I was expected to accompany it. However, I was not always available during those days at Miller Creek, which was three miles from his operation.

Ed talked about his concern and the possibility of being robbed between Sixtymile and Dawson, particularly at a place where an outcropping of rock on both sides of the trail afforded an opportunity to spring a hold-up. In the early 1930s there was very little other traffic along this wagon trail. I told Ed I would investigate and make a report so his concern would be on record.

There was no argument that a hold-up could be easily achieved, but there were only three ways to escape with the loot. The choices were east to Dawson or west to the Alaska border on the trail. The third way, to avoid being seen by a stray witness, would be by water, along the Yukon River. The suspected spot was about halfway between Dawson and the border. The logical route would require the bandit to leave the trail and descend to the river by following a creek bed which might prove hazardous. I had to check it out.

I made a light pack of some utensils, including food and tea, but no bedroll as it was the height of a hot summer. Then I hiked about eight miles up the mountain to a cabin and made myself as comfortable as possible.

In the morning I followed the trail east about 25 miles, where I found another cabin and settled for the second night. Early next morning I reached the point which could tempt an outlaw after gold. Trying to think like a criminal, I left the trail and struck north towards the Yukon River, following a tributary which I believe was Cassiar Creek. I descended easily for a mile before reaching timber, which consisted of stunted pine trees, and managed another mile without too much trouble. Then, as I got into the real timber, I was forced to drop into the creek. This too was easy at first, with bushes on each side and a down-draft of fresh air to keep the mosquitoes away.

A few hours later the growth was thicker and the bushes extended from both banks to interlock overhead, creating a canopy that cut off the fresh breeze. I took out the mosquito net I carried, securing it snugly over my stetson and down my shoulders to protect my face. Then I plunged ahead, but slowly, as it was steeper, and ran into a thick cloud of the pests that pursued me with a diligent hum. A few small ones got inside the net but I left them alone, fearing that if I tried to slap them the main swarm would get through. With vision restricted I struggled on, trying to keep my balance with my boots in six inches of water, although I was on a fairly level gravel bed. It was unexpected torture, stiflingly hot, without a wisp of fresh air. But I had to keep going.

Gratefully I broke out in the clear, leaving the mosquitoes behind in their hot haven, and dashed towards the river, tearing off the stetson and net to face a cool breeze. I splashed in the water, then looked around. A dog barked and I saw a fairly large cabin. A man came around the corner towards me with a look of shocked surprise.

"Where the hell did you come from?" he asked.

"Off the ridge and down the creek."

"In the ten years I've been here, you're the first person to come off the mountain."

I told him I was the policeman at Miller and he said he made a living cutting four-foot fuel logs for the steamers between Dawson and the Alaska ports.

"That's quite a hike," he said.

I told him I had started out early and it had taken all day. One of his kids showed up and he turned to the youngster.

"Tell your Ma to put on the coffee."

The kid ran off and I asked him how often the boats came by. He said there wouldn't be one for a couple of days.

"Too bad," I said. "I want to see the constable at Fortymile."

"We know Alec," he replied. "Stops by on his boat in summer and by dog team in winter."

We started to walk towards the cabin and he told me his name was Olson. Then he suggested I could get to Fortymile by rafting, and when I said I'd give it a try he offered to rig up an outfit. When we reached the cabin I began to realize how tired and hungry I was. Mrs. Olson, bless her heart, had been busy and the most wonderful aroma of bacon and eggs sharpened my appetite. While I packed a heaping dish away, with home-made bread and coffee for ballast, Olson went off to get a small raft. It consisted of two good logs lashed well together and a home-made paddle cut from a sapling. It was now about 11 o'clock, but with Yukon summer twilight there'd be no real problem with navigation. My energy restored, I joined him by the river.

"Let's get squared off," I said. "How much do I owe you for the logs and meal?"

"We never charge a policeman," he replied.

I thanked the Olsons for their hospitality, straddled my "conveyance" and pushed out into the current. Soon I was slipping along at several miles an hour and found it pleasant going after the long day climbing and descending the mountain. I was experiencing another novel way to patrol, but it wouldn't be the last. As I slipped along in the quiet night, I thought about that last bit, for never again in my life would I see such a thick, dark cloud as those menacing mosquitoes. I did very little steering, but kept a sharp eye out for obstacles and had been warned to stay clear of the fast-flowing Fortymile River where it enters the Yukon.

It was three o'clock in the morning when I saw some scattered buildings which I presumed made up the Fortymile settlement. Then I started to paddle furiously and managed to work the cumbersome raft towards them until it grounded and I secured it to the shore. I walked to the detachment building and roused Constable Alec

Unia from a sound sleep. He, of course, was surprised at this unexpected visit and I explained the reason for the patrol as he fed me. Then we retired. It had been a long day.

Although Alec had a well-built cabin, the nights were still chilly and he kept a fire burning in the heater. I hung up my patrol trousers, heavy wool socks and boots, which had been soaked with my legs dangling in the water for balance. After four hours of sleep, I surfaced when the aroma of fresh coffee reached my nostrils, washed quickly and got to the table as Alec served scrambled eggs. It was a mixture of dried-egg powder, water and a dash of Carnation milk. We topped it off with toast and strawberry jam from a four-pound tin which sat on the table in front of us.

Alec and I had met on the trail a few times during the winter, but this was our first get-together in summer. We discussed the purpose of the patrol and the possibility of an outlaw getting through the country I had just travelled. We agreed he wouldn't get very far packing an ingot of gold. We covered other police concerns and exchanged the usual gossip while I helped with the chores. After a couple of days I was fully rested and eager to leave.

Going back, against the fast-flowing Yukon in summer, was no light matter. I wondered if there were alternatives for my return to Miller. Alec solved the problem when he found two young men about to freight a couple of loaded Yukon boats from Fortymile to Jack Wade Creek in Alaska. These are big, double-ender vessels, about 20 feet long and capable of carrying a good ton of cargo. They are strongly constructed but unwieldy, and the boys told Alec they'd be delighted to have an extra set of muscles for the struggle ahead. Although it would be a roundabout route to my base, at least I'd be seeing new country and learning another way to travel in the Yukon.

Hauling these freight boats against the current of the Fortymile River was not an easy task, and every man on the job had to be either an expert or a very quick study. They used a "headline," a long, half-inch rope which ran from the bow to the stern. I watched them start out, walking along the bank pulling on the rope and I followed alongside, studying their technique. To adjust the attitude of the craft as it attacked the current, the man with the headline manipulated his rope. If he wanted the boat to veer away from shore he slid his hand astern and the bow turned away; by pulling the bow end tight he brought it heading towards the shore.

It took a certain amount of practice and water sense to perfect, hauling a deadweight every step of the way, and it was a slow, laborious job. I was grateful, having the opportunity to learn the art from experts, and they were glad to have the extra muscles so they let me practice in calmer water. But just as I was getting the hang of it, we came to the rapids.

To navigate the rapids we beached both boats. Then all three of us tackled the first. The most experienced boatman took the headline and began pulling, while two of us waded into the churning water, waist deep and sometimes more, keeping the pressure up while fighting the current. When we came to large boulders we had to force the craft around outside them while the headline was kept taut. After we had the first boat through and had rested, we returned for the second. Back to steady towing, I was rewarded when they let me try the headline again.

At the end of a long day we stopped to scratch up a meal and rest for a few hours, lying on the sand in the summer twilight. We worked on until late the next afternoon. Just as I was beginning to flag, we came to the gold-mining settlement of Jack Wade Creek, a few miles inside Alaska, and the task was completed.

As soon as we had delivered the freight, we headed for the roadhouse, where we tucked into a great, home-cooked meal, and I lost no time climbing blissfully into bed. After a full night's sleep in unforgettable comfort I was ready to hit the trail again. Thanking my young companions for the opportunity to travel with them, I swung pack on back and headed up the creek to the mountain trail. It ran between Chicken Creek, Alaska, and Dawson. I had to watch for the markers at the international boundary, then start looking for the right path or trail that would take me down the south side of the range.

I started down what I estimated should be the right place and fortunately it led to Miller Creek, which emptied into the Sixtymile. The path was little used and poorly marked, but when I reached the area where miners had been operating I found a decent trail to walk on. I picked up the pace as I sensed the familiar landscape and reached the detachment to a joyous greeting by the dogs who had been looked after by friends. I had enough energy to give them a little extra attention and their evening meal. Then I rested for a couple of days.

Eventually I hiked the three miles to Holbrook Dredging to give Ed an account of my survey. After I had described the country and the obstacles in the way of the third escape route by water, he agreed it would be almost impossible. Even a hardened mountain man could scarcely pack 50 pounds of gold that far. I mentioned the hazards of mosquitoes, and detection by the woodcutter's family and dog. I managed to set his mind at rest and he saw that it was not practicable. All this I included in a detailed report which went on record at headquarters. A copy would be on file at the detachment, and might be of assistance to one of my successors in some emergency.

No hold-up has ever been attempted in this area, either during or after my time. Half a century later I drove from Dawson to the border over the same old mountain trail and found it hard to believe. I began to wonder if my memory of the early days was slipping. Curves had been straightened, the road was wide, gravelled and well graded and it carried a proud, official title—"Top Of The World Highway."

Would anyone but an old sourdough believe me?

Emergencies

CHAPTER EIGHT

*A*fter visiting all the lonely cabins and pockets of activity in my district that first winter and perfecting my handling of the dogs under changing weather conditions, I had a better understanding of my duties. One thing was abundantly clear. The detachment at Miller was not in the most efficient place to serve the whole area. I made a report to the officer commanding, requesting a transfer of the post to Sixtymile, from which point I could more easily reach the boundaries.

This was quickly approved, to the satisfaction of my friend Ed Holbrook, and the Holbrook Dredging Company constructed a large, two-room log cabin which they leased to the force. It was located some distance from the residential area but close to the intersection of the main trails. I lost no time moving in.

Towards spring of 1934 I had occasion to visit Dawson just in time to catch the annual fever of predicting when the ice would break up. It was an event which had been going on for years and meant the end of the long winter, and the arrival of the first boats with people, news, fresh vegetables and fruit. Everyone able to count is willing to gamble on guessing the exact time, to the day, hour and minute when the mighty Yukon will come out of its winter sleep and start moving explosively towards the Bering Sea. The inhabitants of Dawson registered their "guesstimates" ranging from the last week in May to the first week in June. These were entered on wheel charts in various business establishments and ranged from 50 cents to five dollars. The winner would be the one closest to the exact time.

That was recorded at Jeanerette's Jewellery on Queen Street, a few yards from First Avenue, more commonly known as Front Street. It was an ingenious, complicated hook-up. A tripod frame was erected and set firmly in the ice near the centre of the river. From it a cable ran to Jeanerette's store via the Bank of Commerce building on the river bank at Queen Street and First Avenue. When the tripod moved to stop the clock, the official time was established.

A few warm days would excite the gamblers and it was not uncommon to see a group of citizens lining the river bank. Always there'd be someone who thought they saw it move, and even if the tripod trembled or shook it might not be enough to stop the clock. The tension would continue to build, and more characters would appear, for it was an emotional time in the north as well, with the promise of release from the grip of winter.

I could not wait for the result, because it would mean I'd be trapped in Dawson for weeks. With the break-up, ice and debris would block all river traffic, while melting snow would temporarily close the summer trails. I had to leave for Sixtymile, putting off my departure until the last moment in case anyone ahead had trouble on the trail and I could help.

The dogs, who had rested long enough and demanded attention, could sense my preparation and communicated their excitement by bouncing to their feet and snapping out of their kennel lethargy. As soon as I gave the command they were off, heading for the river bank and onto the ice, up the Yukon towards Swede Creek. I had the usual problem here with surface water and snow dams, but the dogs were able to cope except in deeper spots; there I was able to help by pushing the sleigh while they tried to keep their footing.

We were ready to stop when we reached the cabin at the divide leading to California Creek, having covered 40 miles. After getting the animals settled I started a fire, unloaded my things and made a pot of coffee with melted snow. The aroma went well with beans and bread soaked in the liquid, but it was a sudden change from the life in barracks. The soft bed was exchanged for the simple cabin bunk built with unbending poles. But I had logged miles of experience and crawling into my sleeping bag I was soon fast asleep.

Next morning we had easier going from California Creek to the Sixtymile valley, but from there on the travel was tougher. We ran into patches of bare ground which acted like a brake on the runners and the dogs had to take up the strain. When we reached the Holbrook camp in the evening of the second day out of Dawson, the dogs

were extremely tired. They showed it most significant-
ly by the droop in their bushy tails. As I settled them
in their kennels I was hoping that, after a heavy winter's
work, they would now be able to rest until next fall. They
needed to build up energy and stamina before they faced
another long winter.

I had just got a fire started to heat water for a good
wash and was unpacking the load when I noticed a figure
coming from camp. Someone had spotted the smoke from
my chimney and I let out a groan, for the last thing I
needed was a visitor. It was Ed Holbrook himself and
my attitude changed, for he had done me a favour or two.

"Ed," I said with a smile. "Come on in."

"Can't visit. We've got a very sick man in camp.
Needs help."

"Accident, Ed? How bad?"

"No accident. Vic Foley's got a badly infected arm."

"How come?"

"Driving those 12-foot pipes into the permafrost."

"Are you taking him to Dawson?"

"Team's stuck in town and Vic needs help now."

I went back to the camp with Ed and examined
the patient. Vic had an ugly-looking right arm, swollen,
with veins discoloured. It looked to me like blood
poisoning. He had been driving iron pipes with a sledge
hammer to help thaw the permafrost. This had raised
blisters on his hands which broke, and huge callouses
had formed. I decided no time should be lost getting
him to hospital.

"My team needs a couple of hours to rest. They've
had a rough trip. But I'm game to try."

"I'd be grateful, and so would the gang."

"Get Vic ready to leave later in the evening when

the frost has firmed the snow and ground between here and California Creek.''

I repacked the carryall and threw dry clothing into a dunnage bag in case we went through the ice without warning. I added a double-bitted axe and snowshoes, because the weather could turn vicious. The last thing I packed on top were sleeping bags to give the patient some degree of comfort. As I slowly went about putting the team into harness, the dogs showed very little joy and I shared their mood.

We started shortly after midnight and plugged away at a steady pace until we reached the cabin at the divide. While the dogs rested I made a fire and a pot of coffee. Vic did not want to eat, so we finished the coffee and were on our way again while we were still warm and loose. It was an easy downgrade to the Yukon and gave the team a break they needed. It also gave me time to worry about what I would do if the ice had gone out, for I had to get the patient across if he was to reach the hospital.

As we neared the mouth of Swede Creek I was most relieved to see the ice still firm on the river, but there were large patches of water along the shoreline. Here the snow had disappeared, forcing me to drive the dogs through the water to take advantage of the smooth ice underneath it. It wasn't the best thing for their feet, but it was the easiest work for the load they were hauling.

I travelled north, looking for a safe crossing. About a mile from Dawson I found an area free of water and smooth as a sheet of glass. We slithered across and managed to follow the river bank on the ice almost to the business section of town before we hit bare ground. Then it was at least half a mile of tough sledding to the hospital. The team struggled gamely, knowing they were on the last lap.

The hospital, on a high rise of land, gave the staff a clear view of town and someone must have spotted us struggling up the hill. It was late afternoon or evening, but when I halted at the foot of the steps there was a sister to lend a hand, and she helped Vic while I looked after the team. When I was able to enter I found Vic with his arm in a vat of hot water. I gave the staff what information I had, then got to a telephone and called headquarters. After reporting the circumstances, I advised that I was leaving immediately to attempt a return to Sixtymile.

I had checked the paws of each dog, for I had noticed the odd spot of blood on the trail before we entered the water. At this time of year the snow crystallizes and punctures the skin between their toes. At each stop, if there was trouble, they would lick their paws, but I found that the last run through town in soft mud had packed any cuts and they were ready to travel. There was one more obstacle. As we were moving along Front Street I called for the leader to turn down for the river. Miller looked back over his shoulder and went straight on. I called again; he looked back again and continued heading towards the barracks and the kennels. He must have thought I was crazy, going back on the trail. I seldom used the whip, but I reached for it and cracked it just above his head with my final order, "Gee." Miller realized I meant business and he turned to descend to the ice.

We struggled slowly back along the trail through the spring evening, painfully tired and hungry, literally with our tails between our legs. I was determined to reach that cabin on the divide. The last miles were like a bad dream and it was an effort to feed the dogs and grab a bite myself before collapsing on the bunk. In spite of my training, I was too tired to replenish the woodpile. It could wait until morning. We had been travelling for better than 24 hours, and had covered approximately 120 miles.

We were late getting away next morning for I had to complete the chores I had neglected. We started out slowly in a tired, trance-like state, but I felt relaxed, knowing we were safely in our own territory and not trapped in Dawson. I was also cheered by the knowledge that we only had another 40 miles to go, even if it meant sloshing through water on California Creek and the Sixtymile before sliding through mud on the last part of the trail, and that Vic was safely in the hospital. The dogs looked bedraggled and their coats did not have their normal fluffy appearance. When called upon, they had given their last ounces of energy and I felt sorry for them. It was like punishment they had not deserved. I more than appreciated what they had done for me and I tried to show it when I fed and fussed over them.

When we reached our own haven and the dogs were settled comfortably, I got my fire started and began looking after my own well-being. The smoke quickly sent news to the settlement that I had returned and several men hiked over for details, anxious for Vic's safety as he was very popular.

None of us at Sixtymile knew when the ice went out or who had won the sweepstakes until the Holbrook company dog team arrived from Dawson four weeks later, having broken the trail over the ridge. The details that filtered through grew more and more interesting.

The ice had started to lift while I was approaching Swede Creek on my return. Soon after I had left Dawson and made it across, the water was observed rising at the banks. There was an eruption in the centre, throwing large chunks of ice into the air, with sounds of cracking and grinding followed by the roar of the Yukon in headlong spate. This sound could be heard for several days.

I had all the proof I needed that it had been a close call, and this left me eternally grateful to my young, four-legged pals for getting me through at a crucial time. As the excitement of the river returning to life subsided, everyone in town acquired a new interest. When would the first steamer arrive from Whitehorse with returning Yukoners and fresh produce?

Two months later Vic Foley returned to camp, fully recovered. He received a big welcome from his friends, and when things settled down he came over by himself to see me.

"You know I was damn lucky," he said, and wanted to talk.

All through that desperate trip, racing the clock, Vic had hardly uttered a sound. Now the words spilled out.

"I never prayed before, but when we went down Swede Creek, if the ice had gone, I knew I was doomed."

"Don't think I wasn't worried, Vic. We wouldn't have had a hope in hell of reaching the hospital."

"One of the nurses told me they caught the blood poisoning just in time."

He then went into details about how the doctor had managed to save his arm and possibly his life. He wanted to know how much he owed for the transportation, as he was fully aware of the risks we had taken. I tried to explain it was just a duty, expected of me; the real reward was being able to report a successful mission.

He wasn't satisfied, but went away. He became an embarrassment, because every time we met he raised the question of his debt. He was bound to continue; then I remembered his past. It was well known he was a retired boxer, professional enough to have fought in New York for a world title. The next time he brought up the matter of debt, I asked him if he could find time to give me some lessons, teach me the proper art of boxing. His smile was enough to show how pleased and eager he was to repay a debt by doing something he loved.

He came to the detachment regularly, bringing his boxing gloves, and we worked inside the cabin after moving the furniture around. He started by showing me the correct way to stand, left arm extended and both hands cocked.

"Let's spar around. I want to see how you move," he said.

I waved my arms about and he told me to shoot a left. Then the lessons started, and when he had me correctly shooting a straight left, he introduced the feint. He had me starting for the head, but going for the stomach, then hooking and counter punching. This went on as regularly as we could manage when I was not away on patrol.

He then worked on my condition and we went jogging. Vic carried a whistle. At a signal I would leave him and run flat out until he blew it, when I'd stop. He would see how long it took before I got my wind back. He had me going in spurts, as I would in the ring between bells.

We began to spar more seriously as my timing improved and he caught me a time or two and rattled my teeth. I managed to catch him more than once and he swore that I had been trained before, but the truth was that I was catching on and really enjoying it. Then he wanted to test me by having me take on one of the boys in camp who had some experience in the ring. I felt that it would not be a good idea, however it turned out. It was quite enough to feel confident that I could handle myself in self defence with a man of any size. Vic had more than repaid any obligation he felt, and I told him so.

He thought I should turn professional, leave the force and make a career of it.

"I can get you a fight in Whitehorse with a guy from the States," he said.

By now I loved the outfit, the work and the way I had been trusted and treated. Gently but gratefully I declined the offer. Vic Foley did not visit me again.

I had another hazard of my own to face at Sixtymile where the log cabin was not too well insulated. When the temperature hung between 60 and 70 below for a week, I had to keep the heater well banked through the night. Being a light sleeper, I was awakened one night and I surfaced slowly to an unusual noise. I tried to analyze it, then I glanced at the ceiling and was horrified to see a small, red glow several inches long between the roof poles. In seconds I was into clothes and up the ladder to the roof. The snow near the chimney had melted and the soil was dry. When I pulled it away, the moss was alight for several feet. I quickly scooped snow to smother the fire, then pulled the moss from between the poles to make sure the fire would not restart.

By the time I returned to the cabin the fire in the heater was low, but I wasn't taking any chances by reviving it. The cabin was still warm when I crawled back into bed, but the cold crept through the crevices and silently began to lower the temperature. I lay awake the rest of the night, trying to keep warm, shivering under the blankets. I stared at the roof, waiting for daylight to show in the open spaces between the roof poles.

As soon as there was enough light I dressed hastily, climbed back on the roof and stuffed the holes with cloth which I then covered with snow. Then I fired up the heater and when I was warm again I went outside looking for frozen soil. I'd break off a chunk, bring it in to thaw, climb the ladder with it and place it over the bare poles which I had chinked. Then I shovelled more snow on the roof to cover the soil.

If I had not been a light sleeper and the roof had ignited, the best I could have done was to throw outside as much of the contents as I could before the roof caved in. Then my only hope would have been the team and a dash for help on short rations.

In the spring of 1935 the residents of Sixtymile were enjoying the warmth of the returning sun as it melted the last pockets of snow on the lower levels of the hills. The valley had been free of snow for several days and the run-off had found its way to the Sixtymile River which fed the Yukon. I too was enjoying a peaceful spring day. I had travelled hundreds of winter miles with my dog team, visiting the outposts, and now I was looking forward to an easier time with the passing of winter's grip.

Having shed winter clothing, I was puttering about the place, cleaning up around the kennels and performing necessary maintenance to make the place presentable before starting out again on foot patrols. That included dog faeces and bits of wood and bark revealed by the melting snow.

The police building was isolated, about 500 yards from any of the mining company buildings, for several reasons. We were placed at the junction of the main trails, convenient for travellers to reach in need, and far enough away to avoid the possibility of children playing too close to the idle police team.

Timber wolves had been used in the breeding of dogs for the force, to inject stamina and adaptability to extreme cold. They were trained and used for work without sentiment, and were never treated as pets. Everyone in the settlement knew they had an unpredictable wild strain in them.

That afternoon I decided to walk to the post office for my mail. It was handled by the owner of a mining concession halfway up Miller Creek, about three miles from Sixtymile. It was a lovely day for such pleasant exercise and I started out in great spirits, little realizing that a few hours later I'd be doing an emergency hike to Dawson under distressing conditions.

While I was absent a very small child wandered away from home and found its way to the police kennels behind my cabin, alone, in spite of the distance. By the time the mother realized what had happened and went in search it was too late. She heard her child screaming, ran down the trail and found one of my animals shaking the little one like a rag doll. She grabbed hold of her child and kicked out at the husky, who bit her in the groin. In doing so he lunged, and broke the restraining chain. Things might have been worse if one of the men from camp had not rushed in, grabbed the loose chain and secured the excited animal. Mother and child were taken to the office, where the staff rendered first aid and made preparations for a trip to the hospital in Dawson.

I was horrified when I heard the news on my return from my spring stroll. It was the maverick in the team, half wolf, who was responsible. He had never got along with the others and had a mean streak. I locked the detachment and hurried over to the camp, even more distressed on learning the child was a little girl of about three years. I never knew the parents, a young couple in their twenties, but I think their name was Knox. Mother and child had been tended to and bundled up. A team of horses hauling firewood had been called in, the wagon box was fitted to make the pair as comfortable as possible for the rough trip, and a seat had been rigged for the teamster and his swamper.

While this was underway a second team with another wagon was sent on ahead, taking the difficult mountain trail as far as the first cabin, where they would rest and wait to relay the patients onward.

I joined the first party, and when they reached the cabin I started out alone on the long trek to Dawson after a hearty meal. There were problems ahead and it was my responsibility to overcome them. The summer trail was not a graded road, though a small tractor with an improvised blade had been used to level some parts of the 55 miles of switch-back along the top of the ridge. About halfway to Dawson there was an obstacle that would take more than a home-made bulldozer to remove. That was a solid dome of rock, too smooth for traction, which horses would be unable to climb. I had to reach Dawson, organize a tractor and wagon and return to meet the party at the rock when they arrived there.

The trip was a nightmare which I had to face alone. In parts I encountered snow and about a foot of slush. Then I would run into bare ground, which was muddy and slippery. On a climb, one step forward resulted in my slipping back half a step. It was a slow, discouraging hike and it took me 29 hours to cover approximately 55 miles. When I reached the Yukon River I was just about at the end of my tether, and it was fortunate that the ferry operator lived in a cabin on the west bank. Though he was known as a cranky old cuss, he turned co-operative in this emergency, dressed quickly and rowed me across to the ferry, which had to be kept in safer anchorage on the Dawson side.

While he got the ferry ready I went to the hotel where I knew the Holbrook men stayed. They were in town getting supplies for the summer's work after the spring break-up, and it was not long before they had a tractor and wagon at the river. We loaded and cast off, the operator adjusted his rudder, and the ferry, attached to an overhead cable, worked on the strength of the current.

The tractor moved about four miles an hour, faster than I could walk, but still it seemed too slow in this emergency. However, the timing could not have been better, for we arrived at the rock dome at the same time as the relay team reached it with the patients.

Mother and child were carried carefully over the obstacle and placed gently in the wagon, and I travelled with them to the hospital. The driver did not spare the engine and we had a bumpy 30 miles before I could hand the patients over for proper treatment. I hung around the hospital anxiously until a nurse was able to assure me the injuries were not too serious.

After a couple of days rest in barracks, I set out to walk back to my detachment. I timed my departure to take advantage of a ride part way with a tractor-wagon load of supplies for the Holbrook camp. The first part of the journey, a climb of 5,000 feet, was so steep no one but the driver rode, so I started out ahead and waited at a cabin about seven miles from the river. They caught up to me in a few hours and we clanked along to stop overnight at the 32-mile cabin. It had one bunk built of three-inch poles, a window opening but no window, and a doorway but no door. I think it had been used to start a fire by some ignorant doughheads who had neglected the unwritten law of the Yukon: always leave enough wood and kindling for a quick fire.

The cat driver won the toss and got the bunk. The swamper and I slept on canvas spread on the ground. No one bothered to undress and after a few uncomfortable hours, someone rekindled the fire and primed the coffee pot suspended over the top of the drum stove, and we came to life. Having just left Dawson we were not short of supplies. The swamper, with a heavy leather mitt to hold the frying pan over the fire, produced a surprisingly fine feast of bacon and real eggs with fresh store bread. We made it to Sixtymile in the evening of the second day.

If anyone is wondering how we managed to get the wagon over the rock dome, we didn't try. On the north side of the rock there was a vast snowdrift about 12 feet deep which had been compressed and filled by the winds of winter. In the spring it remained a solid mass with a crusty top. The tractor, with wagon unhooked, lowered its blade and began slicing off layers until it had carved a deep trench. They had no trouble working a cut down until the snow under the pack was solid enough to support the loaded wagon and they eased it through. It would not have been possible for the team to pull a wagon through this area until a cut had been made. It is also quite possible, due to the sharp angle, that the wagon would have tipped over, slewed around or even tumbled down the mountain.

Two weeks later, mother and child returned to their home. They had both recovered medically from the frightful incident, but emotionally the young parents began to feel they could not cope with the hazards of the frontier. They decided to return "outside," which they did as soon as the steamers started the summer run between Dawson and Whitehorse. No complaint was received from the parents over this unfortunate accident, which may have left them with a feeling of guilt for not providing adequate supervision for their child.

Naturally I had worried about the consequences of this episode. Without feeling personally responsible, I was concerned about our image and reputation, when the word spread that a police dog had attacked a small child without provocation.

No Court Case
if Possible

CHAPTER NINE

*I*n addition to the normal and emergency patrols I made between Sixtymile and Dawson, I could come in from the detachment for special occasions. I stayed in barracks but went out in civvies to shop or visit the dentist. One year I asked for permission to attend the biggest event of the year, the annual ball on New Year's Eve. We were allowed to attend in red serge, which helped to make it a particularly colourful party, and made us feel accepted as part of the close community. Every member serving in the Yukon hoped to participate at least once.

On the afternoon of December 31, 1934, I had just finished feeding my team at the kennels and was walking back to barracks full of pleasant anticipation. All I had to do was polish my brass and leather and get slicked up for the party. It was my first chance to be part of the tradition and I was in a dreamy state until I was intercepted by Sergeant Major Davies.

"Watson, report to the officer commanding immediately. Don't bother to change."

"Yes sir," I replied, and turned, marching down the empty corridor to Superintendent Tommy Caulkin's office. The offices were empty as everyone had left early to get ready for the party and I took my time, trying to figure out the reason for this summons. I knocked and entered, surprised to find the O.C. alone in his office, a look of concern on his face. He handed me a telegram.

"Read this," he said, "and then I'll explain."

It was from a trader at a small settlement 75 miles south of Dawson, on an island in the Yukon near the mouth of the Stewart River. It warned that two young trappers who were located ten miles up the White River had purchased a quantity of ammunition. There was talk of a dispute over a cabin in their territory and they were planning to take it by force, if necessary. Their adversary was an older man trapping alone. Quick police action was necessary to avoid a more serious problem. I read the message slowly, then handed it back without comment.

"This isn't in your area," he said, "but my concern is the time it would take to get in touch with the man at Selkirk and he would have to find assistance before travelling to White River."

"I understand, sir."

"If you do not wish to take this assignment it would not be held against you."

Tommy was a gentleman and realized he was asking me to pass up the biggest party of the year. As I hesitated I thought there would be another chance to make the party, but this would be an unusual police experience I would not care to miss.

"Sir, I would be pleased to accept," I replied and I think he expected me to say that. He smiled for the first time.

"Right. Pick any man from barracks. Get to town, select what provisions you'll need and leave at first light."

I turned to go and he grabbed my arm.

"And Watson, remember this. No court case if possible."

I went to my room in the quiet barracks and did some figuring. The distance from Dawson to Stewart and to the cabins of both parties would be about 125 miles. I would allow one day to reach Stewart, which had a trading post, telegraph office, a few cabins and a dock for steamers. The second day I'd spend making enquiries and trying to reach the cabins where the trouble was simmering. With any luck it would take another day to settle the dispute, and two days to return to Dawson, but a lot depended upon the weather, the urgency of the mission and not a few imponderable factors. It was at this point perhaps that all the fine training I had absorbed from Raefe Douthwaite came into play.

Travel time depended upon the condition of the trails. It was ten below, a good temperature to run dogs with normal gear. The main trail to Stewart was well travelled and my estimate was based on these ideal factors. For the team I packed 50 pounds of dried salmon and for ourselves I would purchase enough staples to travel light for a speedy trip. The list included six tins of beans and six of sausages packed in bacon fat, pilot biscuits, 20 pounds of raisins, tea, sugar and powdered milk. Now I had to find the right man for the venture.

I went through the list of men available and considered each name, rating their qualifications in my opinion as average or above average. There were some well-qualified members, experienced enough to be considered in the second category, but one name stood out clearly above the rest.

Constable Reg Sheppard was ambitious, did a lot of running to keep in shape and had a competitive outlook. Around barracks he was a loner who did not mix or encourage close friendship. But he was a big man, well built, and when the others who were off duty hung around barracks, he would be running into the hills, testing himself. I knew he had stamina and courage, but wondered if he'd be willing. I found him still in barracks and told him about the telegram and the job I had volunteered for. He was just as eager as I was to get a piece of the action, excited at the opportunity to make a real patrol. As far as he was concerned, the New Year's party wasn't even in competition. I told him what to pack and he ran off to get ready.

During the night it snowed. A strong wind blasted out of the north and the temperature dropped to 35 below zero. We left Dawson at 5:00 A.M. to find it still snowing and the trail drifted in. It was not an auspicious start and I was glad that Sheppard had volunteered. It would have been excusable under ordinary circumstances to delay our departure but it never entered his head, and on the plus side the dogs, who had not run for days, were excited at getting into their harness and took us quickly from the compound to the Yukon River.

There we found the snow eight inches deep and soon we were running into drifts of two feet. That quickly slowed the dogs and forced us to take turns breaking trail with the four-foot snowshoes. The wind, having swung from north to southwest, started stinging our cheeks with frozen particles, reducing visibility.

The snowflakes gradually became smaller, and then stopped. We plugged along, but at a slower pace, and could only guess how cold it was until our breath started freezing on the wolverine-fur trim on our hoods. That indicated to me it was getting close to 60 below. Our pace now dropped to about two miles an hour which we were able to maintain until, at the end of a long day, we caught a pleasant sight that helped us to quicken our steps.

A single light pierced the dark from a lonely cabin window on the river bank some distance ahead. Smoke was reaching for the sky, straight up, another sign of extreme cold. As we pulled up before the cabin I was whistling in the dark, for I had never been this way before. At the first knock the door opened a crack, then widened as a voice shouted, ''Come on in and let me get the door shut.''

It was my turn to be surprised, for it was Bunny Lilievre, a Yukon Telegraph linesman, and this was his cabin. I had not even noticed the line that ran beside the river.

''Bunny,'' I said, ''that was a darn cold run.''

''It's 54 below on the thermometer outside the window,'' he replied. ''What the devil are you doing on the trail New Year's Eve?''

''One of those things, Bunny.'' He was too smart to ask for details unless I wanted to tell him. His big smile and welcome meant that he was delighted to have company this special night.

"Wait until we settle the dogs, then we can visit."

He took our bags of dry clothing and sleeping bags into the cabin while we secured the animals to bushes close by and fed them, after which they made their own beds in the deep snow. We had not eaten since 4:30 that morning except for a handful of raisins. Though it had been a long, tough day, we had only covered 35 miles. But Bunny lifted our spirits and celebrated unexpected guests with a slap-up dinner that included moose steaks, mashed potatoes and tinned peas. After that we were poor company as fatigue crept up on us, aided by full stomachs and the warm cabin.

"Bunny, we've got to make an early start," I said as I drifted off.

When we struggled out of a deep sleep in the dark, Bunny stoked the fire, dashed outside and quickly returned with a big smile, rubbing his hands with glee.

"Well, fellows, you're going to keep me company a few more days. It's 74 below out there."

"Sorry Bunny, we've got to leave as soon as we finish breakfast."

"Come on, no one travels in that."

I shook my head and he realized I meant business. He figured, without being told, that there must be a good reason and the less anyone knew about our mission, the better chance we would have to spring a surprise. I had never experienced working under these conditions, but I figured there must be a way to handle it. With good headgear protecting our faces we'd be all right. A slight opening, letting small amounts of cold air mix with the warmth rising from our bodies before it entered our lungs, would eliminate the danger of freezing our lungs. To prevent the dogs from over-exerting and gulping too much frost, I'd walk in front of the leader.

Stewart was 40 miles away and with luck we hoped to reach it by evening. The dogs behaved well but made no attempt to run and I soon discovered why. It was so cold the crystallized snow felt like sand under my moccasins. The toboggan could not slide easily and made an ominous rasping sound in protest, as if it was being dragged across concrete. The dogs might have faltered if Reg and I had not grunted encouragement. The air was deathly still and we plugged along with obstinate determination in an eerie world where we were the only living things. We weren't interested in the landscape, but the river valley was crowded with surrounding bush and modest mountains averaging 1,500 feet. When the sky darkened to ink, the stars fairly shimmered in the clear air, seemingly within reach. I had no idea how far we were from Stewart and I began to wonder how long we could keep it up. We rounded each bend hoping for a sign of life. Just as I was ready to call a halt, we thought we could see the outline of a solitary cabin on the west bank, and shortly afterwards a single light could be seen. The adrenalin began to flow and I felt like picking up the pace, but like the dogs, I did not have any reserve energy. Reg admitted later he had felt the same way.

Eventually we reached the cutbank to the cabin and struggled off the river, moving as if in a dream. When we stopped by the door the dogs lay down without an order and I had just enough energy to pat each on the head for a job well done. I banged on the door, pushed it open and stepped in. There was a man lying on his bunk, with a look of complete surprise. He obviously had not heard us arrive.

"Come on in, both of you, and shut the door."

We shuffled in without a word and began to melt the icicles from our eyelashes with warm fingers as our eyes adjusted to the glare of the lamp. We must have looked like apparitions, the light reflecting off the film of ice on our parkas and the frost on the wolverine fur. I quickly introduced Reg and myself, as the stranger began putting more wood in the heater and lit the cook stove. Captain Hanson was our host. In the shipping season he was skipper on the stern-wheelers between Whitehorse and Dawson. In winter he worked as a wood cutter, chopping and stacking the four-foot lengths to fuel the steamships.

"Where did you start from?"

"Left Dawson early yesterday. Made it to Ogilvie and stopped with Bunny at the telegraph cabin."

"You came all that way in this cold?"

"It was tough going, but we have to get to Stewart."

"It's another 14 miles."

While he said this he started rustling up a meal and we shed our garments, struggling out of the frozen parkas and pants and standing them on the floor. In front of the heater we stripped completely; our inner clothing was saturated from the sweat we had generated, as we had not allowed our body heat to escape. When the moisture had reached our outer garments it had frozen them stiff, making our steps difficult. Captain Hanson handed us a pail into which we wrung the sweat from our Stanfields. After a good rub-down, we changed into dry clothing, hung the discards from the roof to dry and sat down gratefully to a feast of moose steak, beans and home-made bread. Our host said he was sorry he didn't have spare bunks, but we were comfortable and slept soundly on the cabin floor in our sleeping bags.

After a solid breakfast we headed out early. The thermometer was still registering 74 below, but we managed to reach Stewart about noon and checked in to the roadhouse for a meal. Then we went looking for the person who had sent the telegram. It was Billy Bamford, the trader, who filled us in.

Two young trappers, new to the district, had a cabin and trap-line about ten miles up the White River. Walter Mittlehauser, an old-timer, lived and trapped farther up. They had told Bamford, when they bought rifle ammunition, that when they went to a second cabin which they had purchased from the public administrator, they found Mittlehauser in possession. The old man claimed the cabin was his and the young men said they owned it until the dispute got to the point when Mittlehauser grabbed his rifle and chased them off. With the ammunition, they planned to return and take possession.

Billy Bamford was an experienced northern man. If his assessment of the situation had caused him to telegraph the force and show his concern, we had no time to lose. However, our timetable had been shattered by the extreme cold and we had to replenish our supply of dog food before striking out. We ran into another obstacle when we discovered these people did not feed fish entirely, but depended upon a supply of caribou for their teams. The annual migration had not come through this route and they were feeding a mixture of rice and tallow to the local dogs, exhausting the supply at the trading post. I was forced to reduce the daily ration by half a pound of fish.

We started out the following day and easily reached the first cabin, finding the two young trappers pleased to see us. They were holed up because one of them had cut his foot splitting wood. They explained what had happened when they found the old man in their extra cabin, claiming it was his.

"He wouldn't let us in," said the older one, "and he wouldn't listen."

"Then he whipped out his rifle and fired a shot over our heads," said the other. "We cleared out fast."

I asked if they had proof of ownership and they produced a document which showed they had purchased the trap-line, cabins and equipment of the missing Harry Hanlon, the subject of my first patrol with Raefe Douthwaite.

It was obvious that these chaps were not experienced sourdoughs so I explained the code and spirit of the north, the importance of co-operation, understanding and tolerance, the way an empty cabin is shared by all.

"Now would you agree to letting the old man use the spare cabin to sleep overnight and cook a meal?"

"Sure," said the older lad, "as long as he admits the cabin is ours."

I told them I intended to bring Mittlehauser to their base and settle this problem, and they agreed to go along with the plan. Then we made ourselves comfortable in the crowded cabin and had a relaxed evening.

We set out next morning to locate the cabin in dispute. When we reached it Mittlehauser had left, but it was easy to follow his trail up the creek. We were moving along without difficulty when the lead dog, Miller, stopped in his tracks. When I reached him he had his head in a wire snare which consisted of a loop suspended between trees at just the right height. Fortunately he had stopped before it had gone completely over both his ears and it had not sprung. I removed it easily but had it completed its purpose I might have lost a dog. At each bend in the winding creek we found one of these lynx snares. It was the work of an experienced trapper. From then on Miller stopped at each snare and waited.

After a few more miles at a slower pace, we spotted smoke curling up in the trees ahead and we stopped to catch our wind. Reg and I had talked about how we would find Mittlehauser and what his attitude toward us would be. Just the year before, the "Mad Trapper" of legend had killed Constable Ed Millen and wounded several others. I also remembered a mental case I had guarded at Dawson who had been isolated in the hills too long. We were going to take as few chances as possible.

"Reg, you stay here with the team while I try a quiet approach. If anything happens to me, don't try to get Mittlehauser. Turn back for help."

As I walked slowly toward the cabin I wondered if he had all his faculties, and how he would react. There was only one way to find out. I tapped on the door, pushed it open and stepped inside. Mittlehauser was picking up the coffee pot from the stove. He turned slowly and acted as if he wasn't surprised to see me.

"I'm Constable Watson," I said, holding out my hand. "Are you Mr. Mittlehauser?"

"Walter Mittlehauser," he said shaking hands.

"I'd like to ask you a few questions about one of Hanlon's cabins."

"Sure. Fire away."

I stepped outside and waved for Reg to come on.

The old boy seemed glad to see a couple of policemen and tried to make us welcome. The cabin was just big enough for a bunk, a small table, a home-made stool and a small sheet-metal heater, which was all he had for cooking. The floor was bare ground and the one small window, with four panes of glass, was covered with grime and cobwebs. A number of traps were hanging from the roof poles and the hide of a lynx was on a stretcher, so I figured the old chap was doing alright. As he sipped his coffee, he apologized for not having more than the one cup, informing us his main cabin was up the White River, and then the story began to unfold.

"How well did you know Harry Hanlon?"

"We both trapped off the White for years, spent many nights together at a pivot we shared between our areas."

"What happened to him?"

"I don't know. Nobody does. He just disappeared."

"Now you've got an argument going over one of Harry's cabins."

"That's right, but the cabin is mine. Harry told me if anything happened to him I could have it, and I've always used it."

"Have you got any proof, a document with his signature?"

"Document? We don't use paper. Just a handshake."

"Constable Sheppard and I have examined documents which show the young chaps purchased Hanlon's trap-lines, equipment and cabins from the authorities."

Mittlehauser shook his head but didn't say a word. I waited a few moments to let it sink in.

"You might like to know your young neighbours are willing to let you use it as a pivot cabin if you acknowledge their ownership."

He did not reply and I had to break the silence.

"Will you come with us to sort out this problem?"

It seemed like a long time before he said he would.

"Are you ready to leave now?"

He poured the contents of the coffee pot on the fire and got a pail of snow to add for safety while Reg left to turn the dogs around. Our guest had the privilege of riding on the loaded toboggan while we ran behind, taking turns hanging onto the rope. The temperature had eased up and I felt at peace with the world. The toboggan broke the silence with a light sizzling sound as it slid effortlessly through the inch of fresh snow that had fallen in late afternoon. As the day wore on the sky cleared, and when night fell, it filled with millions of stars so bright I could have read the print on a paper.

The dogs did not need a command when we reached the main cabin of the young men but turned off the trail and halted at the door. We were all given a warm welcome with the news that dinner was ready, and there was little talk as we tucked into moose stew with canned vegetables, home-made bread and coffee. We continued to relax washing up and then I had their attention as I went over the main points. I explained how Yukoners had to co-operate and that I hoped they would continue the custom. The young fellows nodded and I turned to Mittlehauser.

"How about you?"

"I thought it was my cabin. Harry gave it to me. But if it's not mine I'd like to use it once in a a while."

The newcomers went to the older man and shook his hand, saying they'd be glad to see him using it. Reg and I were relieved but I wanted to nail it down.

While they went into details of their routes I drew a map of the area showing the cabins and trap-lines. I made three copies which they studied and signed, retaining one copy for my report.

We got away early in the morning after a breakfast of steak and sourdough hotcakes. Reg worried about old Walter getting back to his place, but I decided they could figure it out themselves. It was a fine day to travel, the temperature a balmy ten below and the trail well packed. We didn't stop except to rest the dogs once in a while until we reached the linesman's cabin at Ogilvie for another relaxed night with Bunny. The following day we reached Dawson.

After everything had been squared away and we had changed and rested, I was pleased to make out my report. Reg Sheppard had been the right choice, showing outstanding fortitude under difficult conditions. The patrol had been successful.

And Tommy Caulkin would be able to add his footnote, which was bound to include "No Court Case Necessary."

Dogs

CHAPTER TEN

As I recall those years of northern service which, in retrospect, marked a turning point in my life, I must stress the importance of the dog team to the policeman serving alone in a remote settlement. A bond of loyalty and dependence grew between us over the years and my feelings turned into trust and respect for these half-wild creatures who never let me down. Trying to write this on the wrong side of 80, I find it difficult to explain.

If handled properly they worked their hearts out under the most appalling conditions, often on light rations. Working animals they were, never treated as pets, yet I grew to understand why Raefe could not face a final farewell when I took over the young team he had been training. The man responsible for their handling and health was amply rewarded if he was good at his job. The team and detachment man were called upon to face emergencies that others could put off for more favourable weather. I am still being dressed down by old-timers in no uncertain terms for that New Year's Eve patrol.

"Only a bloody fool would drive dogs in 74 below," sputtered a sourdough recently.

"But I was told the case was serious," I protested.

Though that young team earned my respect, they kept me on my toes with their individual temperaments and there were a few times when they scared the hell out of me. I kept them well separated at all times and was particularly careful at feeding times to do it quickly and evenly, for then the wolf shows and etiquette disappears into thin air. Their daily ration disappears so rapidly one wonders how they manage to digest it. Their winter ration was half a fish. I'd break a frozen salmon in two and each piece would average two pounds. In summer when they weren't working, I gave them boiled rice with rendered beef fat, and an occasional piece of dried salmon. Each animal wolfed its food first, and then would try to reach the next one's ration, but their chains kept them apart. Handling each one gave me a chance to read their moods and I tried not to play favourites. I seldom had to use the whip.

The exception was when we were meeting another team on the trail, and closing at a fair speed to pass. Here was the potential for a fight, which was a driver's nightmare. Both teams had to give way on the narrow trail and I had a standard drill. As we got within striking distance I would shout loudly and sharply to Miller, the leader, "Gee!" and crack my long whip over his head on the near side. He would pull off the trail and take us past and the danger would be over in a few seconds, providing the other driver had control as well.

A dog fight is a terrible thing, for then all the wildness of the wolf comes to the surface. It happened to me once and I never wanted to experience it again. I was alone at Miller Creek in the middle of my first winter when a terrible racket shook me out of my sleep. I rushed to the window and looked out on a chilling scene. Sharply edged in bright moonlight were two of my team standing on their hind legs, snarling and going for each other's throats. There wasn't a second to lose. I rushed out in pyjamas and bare feet, grabbed each of them by the collar, pulled them apart and held their heads high at arm's length. With strength I didn't know I had I dragged them over and pushed the first into his kennel. I hauled the other to his chain and snapped it on his collar. When I went to secure the first dog, he was cowering in the back of his kennel and I hesitated for fear of being bitten badly. But I knew it had to be done. Cautiously I put my hand in the entrance and began talking to the animal as I extended my arm and felt around until I had hold of the collar. I dragged him out, secured his chain to the D-ring on the collar and stood back in relief.

Then I realized I was in bare feet, standing in the snow with the temperature between 10 and 15 below. Beating a hasty retreat I regained the cabin, grabbed a rough towel and rubbed my feet until the circulation came back with its burning sensation. It had been a close call.

How they got loose remains a mystery. There might have been a scrap of food or refuse from an old garden almost within reach. One animal might have rubbed the pin loose from the clasp and excited the second animal to manage his freedom. Both were minor members in the team's pecking order, but the result might have spelled disaster.

When a dog goes off its food there is only one conclusion; it is sick. To my horror during one summer all five dogs became ill at the same time. They refused to touch freshly cooked rice with fat. I tried them with their favourite salmon but they turned up their noses. I tried to force rice into them without success and then I began to panic. I couldn't call for help or advice, yet I had to do something. As a last resort I took small, hard pieces of the rendered fat, forced it into the mouth of each animal and saw that it melted and entered their systems.

I kept this up for several days, force-feeding a little more each time. Gradually they started to respond until they began eating small portions of rice and finally shook off their lethargy. I put them into their harness and walked them around the yard to regenerate their muscles. This seemed to put more life into them and as they regained their strength I hitched them to a light pole to drag around, and their appetites returned.

Not having had previous experience, I still wonder what the problem was—if it was distemper or if they had picked up some poison. I was very relieved when their health and spirits returned, but from then on I was even more careful handling them. Keeping their feed ground clean in camp and on the trail, I checked for any stray carcass or foul substance. It was routine to examine their paws for cuts and shoulders for strain.

The only time of year when driving dogs was a real chore was the period when spring tried to break the hold of winter and it wouldn't let go. A patrol at this time of year meant traversing the mountain trail in soft snow from a few inches to a couple of feet deep, then climbs and descents through bare patches of frozen mud. The dogs must have thought I was applying the brake when, in fact, I tried to keep the load moving. It distressed me to see my team having to work under these conditions.

Then I had an idea. During summer patrols I had been surprised at the waste in junk piles beside miners' and trappers' cabins. There were broken wheelbarrows, and I began collecting wheels until I had four that matched, in fair condition. I took them to the blacksmith at Holbrook's and described what I had in mind. He did a superb job of making two axles to fit the wheels which I could then attach to or remove from the sleigh as travelling conditions dictated. I tried them on a dry run in summer when the dogs were not in shape, and they were able to haul 300 pounds of dried fish.

That fall, with winter sneaking down the valley from the mountains, I had an opportunity for a real test. A patrol to Dawson under working conditions, and over rough terrain, would give my idea a good tryout.

The morning I brought the harness out from storage the dogs knew the time had come for action and they performed like kids getting ready to visit a circus. They were jumping up and down, straining at their chains and waving their long, bushy tails like flags. As soon as they were hitched they were moving back and forth restlessly, feeling their collars. Except for Miller, the leader, who was standing quietly in position looking at me for a signal.

With the wheels in place and the brake hard on, I called out "Easy . . . easy" and they pushed their shoulders into the collars. I snapped out "Aaaalright," lifted the brake with one foot and stood on the step. I let the teeth of the brake drag to keep control as we moved out easily and settled down to a good pace.

On the flat the wheels worked beautifully as we left the settlement and crossed Glacier Creek. When we started to climb the dogs were able to walk easily, with an occasional rest. We did not find enough snow to warrant removing the wheels until we were at about 4,000 feet. I quickly switched and we climbed another thousand before we hit the trail between Dawson and the Alaska border.

The dogs were showing signs of stress when we reached the first cabin, tails drooping and tongues dripping, which was normal after the idle summer. I was just as ready to call it a day. While I was preparing a meal, Ole Medby, a prospector, and a young companion arrived from Bedrock Creek, each on skis and carrying a pack. They were heading to Dawson for supplies to take them through the winter and I was happy to have company.

Next morning I put their packs on the sleigh and they skied ahead. It was 25 miles to the next cabin and when I arrived they had a fire going and a meal started, which pleased me for I was as soft as the dogs. While Ole cooked I tried out the skis and helped carry in firewood. The snow, about two feet deep, had a crust and I was surprised to find I could move along without punching through. It might be possible to use skis instead of snowshoes in some conditions.

It was heavier going next day with the snow deep and soft, the sleigh sinking, and the dogs again showing fatigue in letting their tails droop. By the time we reached the next cabin, the team and I were satisfied to call it a day. Again there was smoke rising, a meal ready and the chores shared.

As we started our descent off the mountain the snow thinned and when bare ground showed, down went the tails again in dejection. It was time for the wheels. I fastened the skis and poles on the load and got the prospectors to straddle it. I ran behind until we began to pick up speed, then stepped aboard and hit the brake to keep the loaded sleigh from running into the dogs.

Like a miracle they broke into a run, up came their tails triumphantly and someone let out a whoop. What a lovely sight to see them shed fatigue and with these joyous signals let me know they appreciated the invention. We left the snow behind and fairly barrelled along the last five miles to the ferry.

The dogs and I turned south for the barracks, their tails waving to attract attention while I felt self-conscious, driving through town with this strange, modified contraption. Every person we passed turned to stare and some did a double-take. But why should I care? My dogs were happy.

I pulled up with a flourish in front of the bank a few minutes before it closed. This sort of thing wasn't usually done but I had to cash a cheque. I quickly gave the order "Down—stay" and rushed inside before they closed the wicket. I was third in line when a man tapped me on the shoulder.

"Someone is trying to get your team to move."

Now I was second in line and I hated to lose my place.

"Thanks, but I think they'll be all right."

Still, I was worried as I quickly cashed my cheque and hurried out. Two of the animals were on their feet, ready to move, but Miller, the leader, was lying down, his head turned, watching me for a signal. I could have hugged him but I hid both pride and emotion as I drove away for the barracks. I owed much to this leader, including my life, and I am compelled to describe the incident.

We were on the last days of a long patrol when I came upon a lovely stretch of smooth ice, the full width of the Yukon River. It stretched as far as I could see, covered by about four inches of snow, ideal for travelling. The dogs were just as keen to reach home as I was and began running at a good clip when Miller suddenly stopped and stood still.

Whenever a dog wishes to empty its bowels it will pull off to the side of the trail and the driver quickly calls a halt. This time Miller did not step off and I wondered why. It has been known that a lead dog may decide to misbehave, and to correct this, the second dog is moved into his place. I began to wonder if Miller was trying me out.

When I gave the order to proceed he just took a step to the right. I gave the command to get in line and go. He swung to the left. I tried several times, even cracked the whip above his head, but it made no difference.

I decided to give an order with which we would both be in agreement. The sleigh was pointing south and I gave out "Gee-gee." Miller immediately swung towards the west and headed for the shore. He took off at a fast pace, the team following, and jerked the sleigh around in an arc which whirled me, hands firmly grasping the handles, within a few feet of where Miller had been standing.

I punched through the ice, losing my grip on the

handles, but I was able to grasp the wooden frame and was dragged along, the back of the sleigh in freezing water and I well in to my waist while the front of the sleigh was tilted up. The team kept going, but it was a struggle. The sleigh kept breaking through the ice until we reached the shoreline, where it slid onto thicker ice.

I ran the team for a good half mile so they could shed the water from their coats and legs. Fortunately I had my canvas bag with dry clothing and I made a quick change in the open while the team rested. We stopped at the first cabin on Swede Creek, six miles from the accident and I tried to make it up to Miller. If I had gone to the leader when he stopped and dragged him along, forcing him to go, as I have seen other men do, it might have ended in tragedy. There is no doubt in my mind that Miller could feel through his paws that he was not on firm ice and had the intelligence to find a way to inform me.

This might help to explain the anguish a detachment man has to face when the time comes to part with his team. When my time came I was spared some of the turmoil I think Raefe went through. We had an easy run to Dawson under ideal conditions and made it in two days. Once in a while I felt a twinge, then a sharp pain, in my side but when I stopped to rest it went away. When we reached Dawson and I reported in I mentioned this to Constable Jack Sealey in the orderly room. He thought I had better see the doctor just to make sure.

The only doctor in town was old Doc Nunn whom I had met when I first arrived in the Yukon and we had both been in attendance for Barney West's last days. He put me in the hospital, diagnosed severe appendicitis and operated. When I recovered and returned to barracks my team had gone. Reg Sheppard had taken off with them and was now in charge of Sixtymile. I was spared the parting, but many a time when I try to tell someone about our years together and how the dogs supported me, I simply choke up and have to brush away an embarrassing tear. As an old Irish friend used to say about his women, their kidneys were too close to their eyeballs. I had the same affliction.

Spirit of the Yukon
—Part One

CHAPTER ELEVEN

*A*s I recall those youthful days of service, packed with novelty, mistakes and adventure, one theme keeps recurring. My eyes were gradually opened to a world of tolerance, loyalty, consideration and broad-mindedness that created a unique spirit. I would like to relate examples that were both personal and legendary.

When I reached my detachment after the rough foot patrol during which I had been introduced to rafting down the Yukon and headlining a freight boat up the Fortymile, I was pretty well exhausted. After a good night's sleep, my first thought was to write up the diary and clean up the place. When I glanced at the clock it was 11:30. I just had time to shave before going to lunch at the camp. My appearance was frightful, with nine days of beard, and I was slopping around in moccasins because I had worn out the issue boots, thankful no one could catch me in this state.

Just then there was a knock at the door. I opened it resentfully, to the greatest surprise of my life. There, in the immaculate blue uniform that I had so admired from a distance at the training depot in Regina, stood the tall figure of Inspector Jock Binning. He filled the doorway as I stood frozen, in shock, my heart pounding. All the years the Miller Creek detachment had been operating it had never been inspected and he could see the dismay on my face.

"I am looking for the police detachment," he said.

"This is it, sir," I replied.

"I am looking for Constable Watson."

"I am Constable Watson, sir." I answered, still in shock.

"Do you mind if I come in, constable?"

I stood aside, not only embarrassed, but mortified at my appearance before this noble figure. I could explain my dress, but the greatest concern was the stubble on my face. I had gone into the Yukon after six months of training, well aware of the importance of appearances and conduct at all times before the public. In barracks one could clown and get away with it, but in or out of uniform, before the public, the member had to uphold tradition.

Inspector Binning, a gentleman of the old school, remained pleasant throughout the formal inspection as he examined the diary, inventory and reports pending. He never mentioned the subject of shaving and failing direct confrontation I expected it to be recorded adversely in his report. But he did notice my footwear.

"Do you wear moccasins winter and summer, Watson?"

"No sir, the stitching on my boots gave out during the nine days of rock climbing and wading through sand and gravel."

"Was it that bad?"

"The soles started flapping. When I couldn't secure them with string I cut them off. Finished with little between my feet and the ground."

"Next time you come to Dawson, go to stores for a new pair."

It is interesting to note that from then on, members in remote detachments were issued with two pairs of ankle boots.

The inspector had arrived along the wagon trail from the Dawson ferry in a police truck. His driver was Constable Johnnie Piper. I took them to lunch at the mining company dining room. In the afternoon I was questioned at length about the inhabitants in my district, where they lived and how I managed to reach them, winter and summer. Then, as I did not have any overnight accommodation, I began to worry about their catching the last ferry across the Yukon. This was one of the first attempts to travel the trail by motor vehicle and it was hard to estimate how long it would take.

"Excuse me, sir. I do not wish to see you leave, but I wonder if you plan to catch the last ferry?"

"Of course we do. It was uphill all the way here, so we should make good time returning."

"Sir, I have walked it and I know what you mean about hills. But I can assure you it will seem uphill all the way back."

The inspector called Piper and asked for an estimate.

"I was just coming to report, sir. We will have to leave soon."

"How long will it take?"

"Four hours, sir," Piper replied.

In a few minutes they were on their way and I was left alone with doubts and worries, wondering if I had blown my first inspection. I never did hear anything more and I presume he made allowances with compassion, understanding what I had just been through. Years later he was the officer in Winnipeg who handled the enquiry when I applied for permission to get married. It was his job to ascertain if my fiancée met the requirements of the force. I wondered many times if he remembered our first encounter, which had exhibited the spirit of the Yukon.

Recalling events of 60 years ago, my memory is sharpened by photographs. I realize they were taken in a world different from the one we live in today. My concern is that people may not be able to understand the difference or how the harsh reality of the environment contributed to the fellowship that created the spirit of the Yukon. We lived in a world that the industrial age had not reached. There were no highways, telephones, radio, snowmobiles or helicopters and rarely an airplane. In medical emergencies there were no "quick-fix" paramedics. In the outposts and along the creeks, individuals working their claims were dependent upon each other.

The greatest challenge facing a lone Mountie was to uphold law and order or handle an emergency. He had to assess the situation, understand the ethnology of the community and make a judgement that would be understood by the uneducated. Only in an extreme case could the problem be shifted to a court where the legal system could take over. This might be illustrated by two problems I had to deal with.

The first occurred in the spring after my first winter. I had managed to survive patrols by saddle horse and my first lessons handling the dogs. Riding into Granville one fine spring day I checked in at the road-house and swapped news and gossip with Andrew Taddie.

"Haven't seen Theodore Tomsk for over a year," he said.

Andrew seemed worried, for he threw this in before we had gone through the preliminaries.

"Where's he located, Andrew?"

"Been prospecting the Indian River country."

Granville was at the end of the trail from Dawson, going east along the Hunker Summit. It was a large road-house, for it catered to all the miners in the creeks near by and was surrounded by empty shacks the miners used during the winter season. The Indian River trail couldn't be used in summer as a saddle horse would never make it through the muskeg, and Taddie made sure I realized that. The only way to get through would be a route from Dawson via Grand Forks.

Returning to Dawson I made enquiries. Tomsk had not purchased any supplies in more than 18 months. There was a possibility that he had received his rations, not recorded, from someone travelling the winter road to the Indian River. There were few prospectors or trappers working in this area and no regular freight schedule as there was to Granville. We considered the possibility that Tomsk might be ill, or had died, so instead of a saddle horse we hitched the good team of blacks to a democrat, which is a light wagon, in case we had to bring in a body.

Constable Bill Heron, the teamster, and I left Dawson on a warm sunny morning. The horses were fresh and stepped out at a lively gait. Crossing the Indian River bridge later that day we saw smoke rising from a cabin and we headed for it. There we were greeted by a neatly dressed, well-built man of middle age who looked surprised as he put down his tools.

"Come in, fellows. Long time since I've seen the police this way. Need any help?"

"Looking for Theodore Tomsk."

"He's quite a little ways from here, 15 to 20 miles."

"Have you seen him lately?"

"Tomsk doesn't come this way. Goes to Granville."

"Taddie hasn't seen him for more than a year."

"Come to think of it, I haven't seen him for a long time and he always enjoyed a visit here."

This was Chris Fothergill, who prospected and trapped for a lonely living, kept a tidy place and was so pleased to have company and news from town that he tried to get us to stay. We had to press on, so he gave us directions to the creek Tomsk had been working, warning us it was little travelled and poor country for water. Eventually we reached a fast-flowing stream and stopped while the team tanked up. Bill was all set to keep going, but it was late in the day. I decided that we should camp near the water, with uncertain terrain ahead. The country was somewhat flat, with hills in the distance, clumps of trees and small bushes, and I could believe water would be a problem. I pointed this out to Heron.

"O.K. You're in charge," he said.

Bill tended to his team and I cooked dinner over an

open fire. The cook in barracks had sent us off with a loaf of bread, tins of beans and some bacon. Though it didn't get dark we stretched our sleeping bags on a canvas and I quickly dropped off to sleep listening to the murmur of water over rocks. It had been a long day.

Early next morning I rustled up breakfast with the same rations while Bill watered and fed the team. We broke camp, crossed the stream and followed a poor, indistinct trail, partly overgrown with bushes so that we would lose the track and pick it up farther on. This went on for about 15 miles until we climbed over a divide onto a gentle slope which led us to a faint creek. This confirmed Fothergill's warning of a parched land. The team struggled patiently through bushes and around boulders for a few more miles before entering a clearing which revealed a faintly worn footpath. This led us to a cabin with no smoke or sign of life. There was not even a dog to welcome us; it was a scene of desolation. We halted the team at the door and sat speculating, wondering who would dismount first to explore.

The door opened slowly and a big, white-haired man emerged, between 60 and 70 years old, looking wasted. He obviously had not seen a soul for a long time and he had nothing to say. He just stood and stared.

"Are you Mr. Tomsk?" I asked.

"Yes."

"We'd like to get water for our horses."

"Not much here. Creek's a long way off."

"Bill," I said, "check the stream and tie up. Maybe Mr. Tomsk will let us come in and make a meal."

His surprise turned to pleasure as I carried the grub box in and opened a tin of sausages, the foundation for a banquet in those days. It gave me a chance to look around and assess the situation. It was a typical miner's cabin with pots and pans, a tin wash basin, a little furniture, a few tools, but no cupboards. A shelf held several books and a few small potatoes, but there was no sign of canned goods or food of any description. When I questioned him about this he said he had raised potatoes and had shot a bear. I noticed shotgun shells by his chair and asked how he got it. He said he could not hunt any more because of failing eyesight but had shot this one when it came to his door.

Tomsk himself was a pathetic sight, his well-worn clothes, patched with gunny sacking, hanging loosely on his frame. As we fed him he became more inclined to talk, so we asked why he had not made his usual trip to Granville for supplies. He explained that he had not been able to find enough gold, but he hoped this summer he would do better.

We simply could not leave him there alone under these conditions and suggested he come with us to Dawson where the government could help. He refused flatly, saying he was determined to stay where he was and be a success, and if they wanted to help they could send him some grub.

Recalling that Chris Fothergill had mentioned Tomsk always enjoyed visiting him in the past, I changed the subject. After telling him about events at Granville and Dawson, I asked him if he would like a ride to Fothergill's place with us. Chris wanted to see him and it was time he paid a visit to his old neighbour. Tomsk thought that was a good idea.

We set off in a cheerful mood, stopping at our campsite so the team could water, and reached Fothergill's place to a warm welcome. Chris was a good cook, set a fine table and had a large, well-furnished, comfortable cabin. We were happy to accept his invitation to stay overnight. It was apparent that Fothergill was a successful prospector and Theodore Tomsk was not. I took Chris aside and confided I felt it was my duty to see that the old man was checked by a doctor. He could not be left alone with little food and poor eyesight, but he had turned me down flat. I wondered how we could gain his trust and Chris said he would try to persuade him.

Bill and I turned in early while the two prospectors had a visit. Next morning we were served a slap-up breakfast of bacon, eggs and hot cakes. Everyone was in a better mood and our host had achieved a minor miracle, convincing old Tomsk that he would get all the supplies he needed in Dawson and perhaps the doctor could fit him with glasses so he could hunt again. Chris also assured Tomsk that he would help him back to his cabin on his return. So off we went and when we reached Dawson we drove straight to the hospital where the sisters met us and Tomsk entered on the arms of a cheerful welcome.

He spent two weeks in hospital and then moved to a hostel where the government cared for pioneer old-timers who needed assistance. I followed the case long enough to learn that Theodore Tomsk settled down to enjoy the care and attention with the companionship of other old sourdoughs who had helped create the Yukon spirit. He never got back to his cabin.

I had a different problem with the Lyckens brothers, Louie and Otto. When I travelled the lower trail from the Sixtymile to the police cabin on Miller Creek, I passed within a few feet of their cabin door. They were friendly, but more reserved than the average, guarding their privacy. It seemed a little strange in the Yukon but I made allowances when I did stop to chat. Otto seemed a bit retarded and depended on Louie, who did all the talking. The older brother, in conversation and in action, appeared to be protective, trying to make life easier for Otto. These fellows were not mining; they lived a frugal life, their clothing darned extensively, and they did not do much visiting.

Their neighbours were pretty scattered anyway. The miners up Miller Creek were a mile away, those at Sixty-mile two miles and the prospectors at Bedrock a bit farther, but those distances were not a handicap in the Yukon. I made a few discreet enquiries here and there without picking up anything solid, just the off-hand, evasive indication that the Lyckens did a bit of trapping and exploring.

It didn't add up but I kept an open mind until I noticed something odd in my travels. As I passed the cabins of the hard-working miners I noticed, then I picked up, some interesting-looking tins. Time and again I spotted identical specimens and what was odd was the fact that they bore United States excise labels, showing they had contained one pound of tobacco, but they did not have the necessary Canadian label. If the tax had not been paid, someone was doing an end run, and one of the departments I represented was that of customs and excise.

I had a problem. The closest settlement where this tobacco could be purchased was Jack Wade Creek in Alaska. I had walked that trail, a full day each way including a hard climb, and I could not see busy miners finding the time to make that journey. But the Lyckens, accustomed to hunting in the hills, could easily add a little packing to oblige their neighbours and earn enough to help them survive. If this was a fact, and the district knew I was aware of it, they would be watching to see how I'd react.

As my suspicions led back to the frugal brothers, I began to worry how best to explain my position and their duty without making a legal case. It had to be subtle: successful enough to keep them out of court while at the same time teaching them the law. They might just be completely ignorant, but whatever their attitude I had to resolve the problem so they would end up on my side.

Many of the miners wore special waterproof leather boots that came from the United States. The upper part consisted of one piece of thick but soft leather which gave flexibility above the heel without blistering. They were a great improvement over the ordinary boots which were made of heavy, stiff leather with an extra reinforcing strip over the seam at the back. This caused blistering and restricted movement. I wanted a pair for myself very much and I knew the outfitter at Jack Wade Creek had them in stock. So I called on the Lyckens and asked if they could do me a favour. The next time they made a trip across the line, could they pick up a pair of these boots for me? Louie quickly agreed, so I gave him my size and a sum of money with a little talk on the procedure to be followed, which of course included a customs declaration.

I had obtained a list of prices, duties and taxes on trade goods from Mr. Betts, collector of customs at Dawson. No mention was made of previous trips as I explained to Louie how he would have to declare my boots and any other goods he might purchase for anyone else and add this duty to the bill. They followed instructions to the letter and the others involved cheerfully paid their share, pleased and relieved the problem was solved. The subject that had hung over the district and threatened its peace simply evaporated. There were no more attempts to bypass the regulations as far as the Lyckens were concerned.

The next time I paid them a visit the brothers were more relaxed and I received a warm welcome. I started to take an interest in Otto and one day he called me over, excited as a little boy on Christmas Eve. He wanted to show me his latest toys, which turned out to be a pair of very young timber-wolf pups, only a few weeks old. The boys had taken them from a den up the Sixtymile valley and had kept them alive with a good supply of Carnation tinned milk. To this they were adding meat from the carcasses of animals they had trapped. The pups grew quickly and developed into the long-legged species indigenous to the Yukon; they soon were taller than my sleigh dogs.

The pair grew large and strong until one day Louie reported they had broken away. It was a sad loss and a blow to their scheme to use them for breeding purposes. Up to that time I had not heard of anyone keeping a timber wolf for this. The common practice was for the breeder to take one of his females when she was in heat to an area where timber wolves congregate and stake her out. He would collect her after a few days and with any luck he would have a litter of pups with wolf blood.

I felt sorry for the boys because they had raised these wolves so carefully as pets. Then Louie reported that one of them had returned and I went to see the animal. Curiously, it did not act strange, which we had expected after it had been running wild, but was just as friendly. The brothers were pleased and felt rewarded for the care they had taken. However, a few days later the wolf broke away again and this time it did not return. The call of the wild was too strong. I think they expected it to happen and understood.

What had pleased me about the whole incident was the Lyckens brothers' sharing of interest and trust. I remain convinced to this day that the old dictum "No Court Case If Possible" was the best way to go.

Spirit of the Yukon
—Part Two

CHAPTER TWELVE

*T*he pattern for the spirit of the Yukon had been set in the early days of the gold rush. The give-and-take needed for survival had put its own interpretation on law and order. I remember the story Johnny Rosenberg told of an incident in the early 1900s. The famous theatrical entrepreneur Alexander Pantages was bringing a group of dance-hall girls from Whitehorse to Dawson when the boat ran aground on a gravel bar near Carmacks. Mr. Pantages managed to get his ladies ashore, but not without a soaking. Johnny's father ran the Taylor & Drury trading store and roadhouse where Pantages shepherded his thoroughly chilled and dispirited company. While they stood shivering around the pot-bellied heater waiting for their dry clothes to come ashore, the entrepreneur tried to get hold of some rum so they could have a hot drink.

Unfortunately it was Sunday and against the law. Mr. Rosenberg refused to break it or allow liquor to be consumed with a meal at his roadhouse. Pantages was furious. He was used to getting his own way and bending conventional rules in the untamed frontier where the rule of law was green. He demanded to speak to a member of the mounted police.

A sergeant turned up and after listening to the dispute suggested that Mr. Rosenberg should take a little walk and cool off while he discussed the matter and explained the law to Mr. Pantages. When he returned, Rosenberg noticed the ladies were in dry clothing and enjoying a meal and with it, each had a hot rum. It was never revealed how the rum was obtained, or who had supplied it to the chilled company, but the facts were as follows, in case a report had to be made. The proprietor had followed the letter of the law in refusing to supply liquor on the sabbath. No complaints were received by the police, so the law had been upheld. The ladies survived and Mr. Pantages settled the account for meals, accommodation and service.

I was well aware of the dangers inherent in the temptation to accept a drink. The charge of "Intoxication, However Slight" had been drummed into us. This meant that if you were caught unsteady on your feet, even after a glass of beer "down the road you could go."

At Dawson single men had to be in barracks by 10:30 P.M. Anyone who wished to accept an invitation and come in later had to obtain a written pass from the commanding officer. In those days, members did not visit the hotels to socialize. Not only was it too expensive, it could result in charges under the RCMP Act. However, in that friendly community, established citizens opened their homes to the policemen and passes were not hard to obtain.

One popular constable received regular hospitality from a lady who never let him return to barracks without having a drink of liquor. He never asked for a pass, but faithfully reported "In" to the night guard before 10:30 and would sneak out later with no one the wiser and find his way back to the house of refuge. On his final return in the wee hours he would bypass the guard, and avoid the flying picket doing his rounds and the orderly officer. Generally he got away with it.

If caught, he would plead guilty to being intoxicated "however slight" and when asked the names of other members of the party, always replied "I was alone, sir," which endeared him to all his fellows. He would receive the usual fine of $20, a third of a month's pay, and a warning not to do it again. In all other respects he was well liked and efficient, and upheld the tradition.

One night when I was on duty as night guard this particular member reported "In" at 10:25, chatted for a few minutes, then went upstairs to bed. The guardroom, in a long wooden building, had a side entrance. A person had to walk along the side, mount three steps to a small wooden platform and make a left turn to enter.

It was a quiet summer night, and much later, I was fighting a tendency to doze when this same character managed to mount the three steps, stood swaying to all points of the compass and waved, presumably trying to signal me to mark him "In." I nodded, and waved him away before he fell off the platform. He swayed out of sight and I held my breath, now fully awake, hoping the orderly officer, a strict disciplinarian, was not watching the performance.

I began to puzzle over this strange behaviour until it struck me that at this time of year the night was light as day. He had consumed an extra quantity, had lost track of the time and thought he was reporting "In" before the deadline. I settled back, relaxed, feeling the lucky devil had got away with it.

When the orderly officer arrived ten minutes later, I reported all present and correct. He wanted to know where the flying picket might be and I told him. In a very short time the quiet night was disturbed by muttering and thumping on the stairs. I got to my feet as the orderly officer and flying picket struggled into the guardroom with a body, fully clothed and out cold. He was laid out in a cell and I was left alone for some very uncomfortable hours, wondering just where I might fit into the drama.

When he revived, the constable could not recall any details. The picket had related to me that they found a quiet barracks when they made a head count and everything seemed to be in order until they found a pair of boots stuck out at the foot of one bed. When they pulled the covers off they discovered this chap fully clothed. The system had been violated because he was not fit for instant duty.

The next scene was the orderly room after the charge was read. "Guilty or not guilty?"

"Guilty, sir."

"Which other members were with you?"

"I was alone, sir."

He was fined the usual $20 and severely warned. But he was not recommended for dismissal. The bond of tolerance was strong in the Yukon, in and out of the force, and remains so to this day.

Today's visitor to the Yukon, travelling by airplane, Alaska Highway or cruise ship, can still enjoy the magnificence and awesome majesty of the rugged, untamed frontier. However, I feel sorry that they will miss the characters who swept in during the gold rush and helped establish the spirit of the Yukon. I was fortunate to meet and develop friendships with some of the most colourful individuals before they went out to pasture.

One of them was Apple Jimmy, who was a very friendly person. He always wore a smile and was eager to have a chat whenever I stopped on the wooden sidewalk in front of his Dawson store. We both had fond memories of early days in Winnipeg for starters. I always felt that Jimmy did not need to work for a living but operated his curio store to attract tourists and give him a chance to meet interesting visitors. He was a happy man, smartly dressed, wearing a spotlessly clean apron whenever I saw him. If he was not in his store he could be found in the Arcade Cafe next door talking to Nan or Harry Gleaves, the proprietors. Jimmy always had to have someone to talk to.

Jimmy revealed a lot about his past to me over a period of two years. Long before climbing the Chilkoot Pass in 1898 with a heavy pack on his back, he had come to Canada from Greece. A short, well-built man with thick, wide shoulders, he had joined a construction gang building the railway. Working from eastern Canada toward the prairies he was as good as any man with a pick and shovel. In addition, Jimmy the Greek could speak several languages, which helped him make friends easily, and since the contractors found him useful as an interpreter, he had steady employment.

When the railway reached Winnipeg, Jimmy handed in his pick and shovel and opened a small cafe near what is now the junction of Main and Higgins streets. He said he did a good business until the steel reached a place called High Bluff, a considerable distance from Winnipeg, and his hungry clientele were out of reach. Then he put his establishment on wheels and moved it west, keeping up with the construction gangs.

The early liquor trade with its itinerant bootleggers tended to disrupt the pace of railway construction and the Mounties were called in to help. Their solution was to move all commercial enterprises five miles from the camps, but Jimmy, because of his reputation, was allowed to operate near the right-of-way.

It would have been hard to deny Jimmy. With his quiet disposition and reputation for being a good influence, he had gained the respect of all. He had never been known to turn a hungry person away. Many a starving drifter who was broke returned long afterwards to square up the account with his benefactor. Jimmy's philosophy also had room to forget the debts that were not paid.

He followed the crews to Calgary, and then through the mountains to Vancouver in the early '90s. When word of gold in the Yukon leaked out, he joined the flood headed for Skagway and the trail of '98. He was among the first men to test their physique over the cruel Chilkoot Pass, but with those powerful shoulders he could easily pack the amount of food required by the Mounties before they would allow gold seekers in to the Yukon. It had to be sufficient to last them a year.

Jimmy told me it was at this point that he decided to forget the gold and seek his fortune catering to the hungry crowd of tenderfoot adventurers. He opened his first "fast-food restaurant" on the trail between the mountains and Whitehorse and charged two dollars for pork and beans. The bread was extra.

In Dawson he became one of the most enterprising and astute businessmen, with a restaurant and a gambler's instinct for estimating market demands. The trick was to have the right order of goods on the first boat to reach Dawson in spring. With the right guess he could pick up a tidy profit until the other purveyors received their shipments. It was under these precarious conditions that Jimmy the Greek earned his lasting moniker of "Apple Jimmy" and retained his popularity.

It happened early in the 1900s after an unusually hard winter. The break-up of ice in the Yukon was later than usual. The first ship to reach Dawson unloaded Jimmy's supplies first and these included a thousand cases of apples. The local people, starved for fresh fruit, grabbed them as quickly as Jimmy could hand them out and paid two dollars for each one. Jimmy, of course, slipped them out unnoticed to the children and women free of charge in spite of the frenzied rush. By late afternoon he had nearly $10,000, and though he was feeling mighty good his business sense was still working. The bank was just across the street, and when he had put things away he started over to salt his sudden fortune in a safety-deposit box.

But "retribution," as he called it, changed the picture. Before he had reached the other side of the street and the safety of the bank, a fair-weather friend hailed him and suggested they celebrate his success. Jimmy was steered into one of the famous gambling saloons with its dance hall and bar. The crowd had no trouble making room for the popular Jimmy, for whom the urgency of the moment, and time, took a holiday.

A week later Jimmy showed up at his place of business. The bank had not seen his deposit, nor had the regular customers seen Jimmy. He did not know what had happened to his money, but it didn't bother him for he thought he had never had such a good time. Nobody disclosed exactly where he had spent it, but Jimmy never had any regrets. That is how he earned the title of "Apple Jimmy" and an affectionate spot in the annals of the Yukon. Time and again I was told by the old-timers that Jimmy had won and lost more than one fortune and he always maintained he had as much fun losing as winning each time. Apple Jimmy enjoyed a long and useful life, sharing his pleasure with all and sundry he met through the years. I am glad to have known him as a friend.

Walter King was another well-known and popular character at Dawson, well on his way to becoming a legend before I arrived. Sturdy, about five feet ten inches tall, he was approachable, pleasant in conversation and well educated, and always had a crack of a smile ready to break out. Whenever I met Walter he appeared to be somewhat under the influence of alcohol, but he was never intoxicated in public to the point where he could be called obnoxious. His facial features made one think he had run into some solid object, like a brick wall, particularly around his nose.

Walter loved animals and they adored him. Dawson was famous for its stray dogs during the summer. Owners who worked them hard through the winter turned them loose to fend for themselves. When people started to complain, the authorities attempted to remove them from the streets, which was easier to order than to accomplish. Walter would be asked to help and he cheerfully complied. Any other person would have difficulty getting close enough to a dog to grab one, but not Walter. All he had to do was weave down the street and stand at a corner. All the dogs in sight would go to his outstretched hand. Many of them had a trace of wolf, so it was a sight to see.

I found a photograph of Walter in most uncharacteristic dress, posed on the wooden sidewalk with a cane in one hand and a large black dog in the other. On his head was a top hat, and below the smile an immaculate white shirt with tie, vest and swallow-tail coat. This wasn't the Walter I knew, so I asked inhabitants what event might have caused this turnout. What they told me should be preserved in print.

The governor general of Canada was coming to town. A state visit was a rare occasion in this outpost of the empire, and was guaranteed to generate excitement throughout the Yukon, but nowhere with greater intensity than in Dawson. The king's representative at the time was Gilbert John Murray Kynynumond Elliot, the Earl of Minto. He was due on a paddle-wheel steamer from Whitehorse.

Every passenger vessel reaching Dawson at any time was given a great welcome and every able-bodied person, as well as dogs, turned out. But this was also a royal visit and required special preparations. Some characters started celebrating a bit early in what they thought was a regal manner and one wag suggested they should dress Walter fittingly to meet the earl. He was, after all, the one with the best education and they had a selection of costumes backstage in the dance hall. So Walter was decked out and sufficiently lubricated.

Just as the ship was warped in to the landing, Walter was escorted to the foot of the gang-plank and his pals melted into the crowd. His lordship was the first person ashore and he was quickly surrounded by excited citizens who gave him a warm welcome. They were dressed in their customary outfits while the earl was in glorious regimentals. He looked over the crowd and there was only one person in appropriate dress. The governor general stepped towards Walter and extended his hand.

"Good afternoon, sir," he said with a smile.

Walter's disfigured face broadened into a wide grin.

"Good afternoon," he replied and stood smiling, a man of few words.

The earl, being both a gentleman and a diplomat, could see that Walter was not about to make a speech of welcome. He is reported to have given, in a very pleasant manner, his own introduction to a member of a community cut off from world events.

"I am Lord Minto, representing His Majesty the King of England. Who might you be, sir?"

"My name is King," Walter is alleged to have replied, "and I am King of the Bootleggers."

Walter's voice was strong enough to carry through the crowded waterfront and the fraternity was pleased that Walter had not let them down. By this time the official welcoming committee was able to close in and rescue their guest.

It would appear from Walter's remarks that he was involved in bootlegging but this was not the case. He was a combined handyman and runner for the hotels, whose main job was to take hotel orders for liquor to the government store each day. Walter had it down to a fine art. Instead of combining orders into one trip he made many single journeys, for which he often received a nip from an obliging bartender. Between times he might be found sweeping and dusting lobby and bar.

Walter had attended Queen's University in Kingston, Ontario, and so had Mr. Justice C.D. MacAuley. They had known each other there, yet their lives had taken different paths. MacAuley was highly respected in the judiciary, closely associated with the elite of the Yukon, where he presided in summer, and of Vancouver, where he spent winters. He stood at the top of the pecking order, while Walter was a mere hotel porter; if you couldn't find him in the hotels he would be in the F & F Cafe.

It was inevitable that they should meet at least once in downtown Dawson, and if the judge preferred to avoid meeting, it wasn't Walter's way. At the first encounter, this is how it was reported.

"Good morning, MacAuley, how are you?"

The judge was upset, because the citizens could hear the manner in which he had been addressed and this would not command respect for his mighty office. He admonished Walter and demanded to be addressed appropriately before the public. Walter apparently replied genially that he would respect his wishes, but when they were alone he would call him MacAuley as he had done at university.

Understandably, Judge MacAuley tended to give Walter King a wide berth. A strong odour of liquor hung about his clothing, which suggested that he sometimes neglected to undress when he retired after a busy day. When I first knew him he went out of his way to assure me that he was a law-abiding citizen, always ready to help the police. He wanted me to know that I might find him in unusual places at odd times. The worst tag you could put on him was that of an amiable lush.

I will never forget an experience I had when I was on patrol in Dawson one bright summer night. There was very little to do but check the establishments for regulations and watch out for fire or accidents. It was about 3:00 A.M. and so very quiet that the only sound was made by my riding boots on the wooden sidewalks.

Turning west at the corner of Third Avenue and Queens with the intention of proceeding to Front Street, I stood quietly when I caught sight of a figure of a man riveted in the centre of Queens. As I watched, he swayed to one side, then the other, then backwards and in straightening up nearly pitched forward. Wondering how long he could maintain his equilibrium, I observed him for several minutes.

Between Second and Third avenues there was a lane not quite wide enough for two vehicles to pass and the way this character was shuffling his feet, it seemed he wasn't quite sure there was enough room to get through. Finally he lifted one foot, lurched forward and began to zig-zag between the walls, to keep his balance. I hurried to the entrance as he disappeared from view and caught my last sight of him as he turned and aimed for the back door of the F & F Cafe. It was our Walter heading for the barn.

Some might feel the confrontation between Walter and the earl was a disrespectful gesture, but that was not the intention. It was just Dawson's way to welcome anyone, whatever their station. You could call it the rough side of the Yukon spirit.

As an historical event that has faded in the mists of time, a letter to Lord Minto on November 19, 1903, is interesting. Downing Street informed His Excellency "that His Majesty the King has been graciously pleased to confer the title of 'Royal' upon the North-West Mounted Police in accordance with your recent recommendation."

The announcement was conveyed by the *Canada Gazette* on June 24, 1904, and six months later Lord Minto was made Honorary Commissioner of the Royal North-West Mounted Police.

T. Morris Longstreth had a fitting epigram in his book *The Silent Force.* "Thus by a wave of the royal wand the Force was knighted."

Return to the Yukon

CHAPTER THIRTEEN

After four active years of challenge, adventure and growing friendships, I left the Yukon in June 1936. I had arrived a cheechako and was departing a sourdough, toughened and fortunately with a better understanding of people and how to handle unexpected situations. At least three years of single detachment experience had given me new-found confidence. I was ready and anxious to test my skills in police work, confronting the problems in the big world outside.

When I reported at Fairmont Barracks in Vancouver, the sergeant major lost no time putting me back in line.

"Another northern man," he said wearily. "It takes two years to thaw their brains out."

There I was, starting all over again, relegated to the mounted troop which I thought I had left far behind.

I couldn't believe it and went through days of depression. Here I found some of my fellow recruits from Regina days, still doing stables, riding, taking lectures and doing drills. They had been stuck here all the years I had been alone, running my own show. There was an element of resentment, an understandable attitude of jealousy because I had managed to escape regimental discipline; while they had been slogging I had been doing real police work and had returned with money in the bank.

I swallowed the disappointment and tried to soldier on, but it wasn't easy to take. Then I got lucky. They needed help at Abbotsford for a special job and I was sent there on temporary duty. Perhaps the sergeant major wanted to get rid of me as much as I wanted to escape. One thing led to another and I found myself immersed in crime and drug cases in those less violent, more innocent years. But that is another story.

In those days a recruit could not get married for seven years, and then permission was granted only if the applicant had financial means and the girl of his choice had been checked and approved. In 1929 I had met Mary Ellen Trower in Winnipeg and we had corresponded through my Yukon years. I had been saving my pay, small as it was, and could qualify. Mary Ellen, whose nickname is Nellie, decided that I should apply. We were married in Vancouver on March 17, 1939, and set up housekeeping in Abbotsford.

Over the years she has suffered her share of my stories about life in the Yukon, and I dearly wanted her to see the country, to meet and understand the people who had meant so much to me. As my career outside took on more responsibilities, we never had a chance until I retired.

Then, in 1963, we drove north, packing a tent and camping along the way. The war had left striking changes. The Alaska Highway had made ordinary travel possible for vehicles and tourists, with service stations, restaurants, motels and campsites. These changes could not disfigure the panorama of mountains, lush valleys and teeming rivers, or change the people. I wanted particularly to look for old-time friends, those who were left, to have Nellie meet them and discover for herself why they had got into my blood.

When we stopped at Dawson, Ole Medby, who had been a prospector in Bedrock Creek, tapped me on the shoulder.

''Tich, is that you?'' he said, and the memories came flooding back.

We lost no time getting to Sixtymile and it had changed considerably. But I found Billy Williams' dredge at the mouth of Glacier Creek, surrounded and buried in bushes. Billy had leased it to the Holbrook Dredging Company, but it had not been operating for years. Joe Myers, the postmaster, was living in the cabin Billy and his wife had used.

We drove on, a bit disappointed, for it was not the thriving little community with single miners on the creeks, but we cheered up when we got to Miller Creek. There was Otto Lyckens in the old cabin at the mouth of Miller, living alone but able to hang on with financial assistance not available in the 1930s. His hunting days were over, but he kept active growing vegetables in his little greenhouse. Louie had passed away, so Otto was terribly excited at the surprise visit and showed his pleasure in many ways. Nellie really liked him and they got along famously with her interest in his horticulture and the way he managed to keep busy. Otto seemed to have thrived on his own and I began to revise my opinion of his being retarded. Perhaps Louie had been over-protective and when left on his own Otto discovered he could think for himself and make his own decisions. He wanted us to prolong the visit, but I had to see the spot where the old police cabin had stood when I first saw the country with Corporal Douthwaite. We promised Otto that we would drop in later on our return.

The site of my first detachment on Miller Creek was very much alive but the cabin had gone. Ole Medby had a crew of five working a successful mine. It was an interesting visit, reminiscing and watching the present generation of miners while Nellie began to actually see the processes I had tried to describe. We had to get back to Otto, but before we left one of the miners went down the shaft and emerged with four lovely frozen moose steaks from nature's refrigerator in the permafrost.

Otto was primed to talk and though almost 30 years had passed he was able to recall many highlights. During our absence at the Medby mine he had had time to think of incidents he wanted to tell Nellie and they bubbled out in chunks. He even surprised me with events and moments I had long forgotten. It turned out to be one of the happiest days on the trip.

There was no stopping Otto when he was warmed up and with a full head of steam he realized how interested Nellie was. When he began to recount the time Ed Holbrook asked me to try out his new .270 rifle I had to take over, for Otto only had the beginning and end.

Ed had challenged me to prove my skill as a marksman as he handed me the rifle loaded with six cartridges. I had just come in from a light patrol and on the last day had spotted a small herd of caribou not too far from camp. I quickly harnessed the dogs to the sleigh and took off, determined to show Ed that I deserved the crossed-rifles badge I wore.

Between Glacier and Miller creeks I located the herd high on a ridge. I was on the north side of Glacier and the animals were halfway up the mountain on the south. They were a long way off, grazing slowly and blissfully unconscious of any threat. I felt if I moved any closer they would spook, so I signalled the dogs to drop down and stay. They were glad to have a chance to rest.

I worked my way alone, over a draw and up the slope until I was about 200 yards away. Then I studied them. They would graze a spot in a group, then move to another patch of feed and group again. Just as I settled in position, the leader started walking up the mountain, looking for another spot to graze. It was a long shot, but I took a bead and steadied, then squeezed off a shot. The leader stumbled, then dropped.

The herd stopped moving and stood transfixed. Still a distance from them, I decided to aim a little higher and with the next four shots I dropped the animals cleanly. I saved the sixth shell in the event the first animal was not dead.

It took me a while to walk down the north side to Glacier Creek and climb up the other side, where I found four dead caribou and one wounded, which I quickly dispatched. I gutted the animals and stretched them open, taking a chance that wolves would not be so close to a settlement.

When I returned early next day the carcasses were frozen and I had no trouble hauling two animals at a time, one on the sleigh and another dragging behind on a rope. On each trip I left a caribou outside the cabin of the oldest miners on the creek. Jim Bungate did not qualify, for he was the youngest miner in the district and able to hunt his own meat, which he did each year successfully. Ed Holbrook was pleased when I told him what his rifle could do. I kept the fifth animal for my own use.

It wasn't easy for us to leave Otto, but we had to push on to other reunions. He loaded us with fresh lettuce and spring onions and waved us on our way until we were out of sight. On the way to Granville I pointed out the roadhouse at Hunker Summit which had been run by Mr. Fournier. I had regularly stabled my horse and stayed overnight there.

As I drove along the wagon road down Dominion Creek I remembered another character with particular affection. Pete Nazareno had been a successful miner in 1934 in this area. I doubted that he was still alive, but I wanted to locate his old cabin. To my great delight and surprise there he was, as active as one could expect for a man well into his eighties. He was pleased as punch that anyone could remember him and the early days. He was not mining, but preferred to spin out his days in the old cabin rather than in a Dawson hostel. Nothing had changed in his set-up and I was able to show Nellie what old-time spartan comfort was really like. Pete asked if I remembered his special sleigh which he used to gather firewood for the winter. He would lug it up the hills, cut the wood and load the sleigh, then guide it back down with a "gee" pole to steer and brake the run. I wondered if the force was keeping an eye on the old man and how long he could maintain his independence.

Farther down the road I found one of the Troberg boys working a claim with a crew of men. They were using a "cat" to push loads of thawed gravel into a very large sluice box. We watched them make a clean-up, taking a coconut mat from the sluice box. It was carpeted solid with bright, yellow gold, a lovely sight. The treasure was placed in a strong box for processing later.

I brought up the question of Pete Nazareno living alone out there. At his age, I suggested, they should keep an eye on him and check up once in a while. I was told not to worry about Pete. He was still fairly active and a bit touchy about his independence. Every morning they made sure that smoke was coming out of his chimney and they also saw that his supplies arrived promptly from town when he needed them. I pointed that out to Nellie, pleased to find the spirit of the Yukon was still alive.

Writing this today in my eighties, living comfortably in Victoria, British Columbia, I still feel the tug of the Yukon. It continues to draw me to gatherings of the Sourdough Association in Vancouver, Qualicum Beach, Nanaimo, Whitehorse and several places in Washington and Oregon. I find it difficult to define what the north does to the individual, but even today I suspect something happens to broaden the senses and awaken the feeling that we do not stand alone in a lonely environment. There is always someone ready to help when needed and individuals grow in stature thinking about the welfare of their fellow man.

That is what I hope this memoir shows.

Christmas Dinner, Dawson, 1932. Front from left to right: Corporal Douthwaite, Sergeants Cronkhite, Johns, Purdy. Author "Tich" Watson stands behind Sergeant Purdy.

Postscript

HOWARD HOOPER CRONKHITE

Sergeant Cronkhite, a machine gunner in World War One, joined the RCMP in 1920 and served in the Yukon from 1923 to 1935. He was commissioned in 1940, returned to the Yukon in 1943 and was instrumental in upholding Canadian sovereignty when the U.S. Army was punching the Alaska Highway through the Yukon. After serving another five years in that post he took command of "G" Division, responsible for policing all of Canada's north, and was promoted to superintendent. He died in Ottawa December 28, 1949, age 51. He was buried with full military honours and many tributes for nearly 30 years of service.

RAEFE DOUTHWAITE

Corporal Douthwaite served five years in the Yukon, and three years aboard the famous RCMP vessel *St. Roch* in the Arctic. In 1940 he joined the Canadian army, was commissioned and served in North Africa, Sicily and Italy. He landed in Normandy on D-Day as a captain in the Intelligence Corps and joined the French and Dutch underground to comb out German agents. As a spy catcher he won the MBE, French Croix de Guerre and Dutch Order of Orange Nassau. Promoted major, in 1946 he was in charge of Intelligence, Western Command. He died in Halifax October 29, 1990, age 83.

About the Author

onstable J.B. (Tich) Watson came out of the Yukon to serve in British Columbia. He attended Police College at Regina in 1941, was promoted sergeant in 1947 and was a senior NCO at the time of amalgamation with the British Columbia Provincial Police. After his service in the Yukon he returned to England on leave every two years to see his mother, sister and brother until his mother passed away. He retired to pension in 1952 after 20 years of service.

The Watsons started a small nursery on Vancouver Island along the side of the old railway bed which today is the Patricia Bay Highway. When he retired from that in 1962, Jack Watson took up painting as a hobby and began teaching members of the Multiple Sclerosis Society. This grew to a class of 12, and helping them control brush and paint on canvas proved to be a rewarding and fascinating experience. He also found Vic Foley in a hostel south of Vancouver and took him to a reunion of sourdoughs where the old-timer from Sixtymile received a warm welcome.

More than half a century after making the patrol at 74 below zero for "No Court Case If Possible" he finds himself living a mile away from his former partner, Reg Sheppard. Bunny Lilievre, who became a successful business man in the Yukon, married the former Alice Burkhard of Dawson and they are living near Nanaimo, 80 miles north of the Watsons.